Interpretation
of Balance Sheets

LANCASHIRE POLYTECHNIC
LIBRARY & LEARNING RESOURCES SERVICE

This book must be returned on or before the date last stamped

TELEPHONE: PRESTON 262313   SHORT
LOAN

		24. APR. 1996		-3. DEC. 2004
-2. DEC. 1991		TALIS		
-9. DEC. 1991		1 2 FEB 1998	:9. NOV. 2005
-2. MAR 1992				
19. MAR. 1992		TALI		
		- 6 MAR 1998		
-4. JUN. 1992		12. MAY 2000		
IX. 30.				
17. MAR 1993		22. NOV. 2000		
-2. JUN. 1993		16. MAR. 2003		
21. NOV 1994		-1. NOV. 200		
17. MAY 1995		-8. NOV. 2004		

D0278405   71

Also by L. S. Dyer FIB

Balance Sheets and the Lending Banker (6th edition 1986)
J. H. Clemens & L. S. Dyer. Europa Publications.

Bank Lending: with management accounts and case studies (1981)
L. S. Dyer, P. Geerbrant and A. Jollife. Waterlow Publishers.

A Practical Approach to Bank Lending (3rd edition 1987)
L. S. Dyer. The Institute of Bankers.

0852971761

BAR CODE No. 1989471

CLASS No. 657.33024332 HUT

15 AUG 1991

11/2/87

LOAN CAT SL

ii

Interpretation of Balance Sheets

Sixth Edition

by

H. H. Hutchinson, F.I.B.
and L. S. Dyer, F.I.B.

The Institute of Bankers

First Published	1955
Second edition	1963
Third edition	1967
Fourth edition	1972
Fourth edition (revised)	1977
Fifth edition	1979
Fifth edition (revised)	1981
Sixth edition	1987

This book is copyright under the Berne Convention. All rights are reserved. Apart from any fair dealing for the purpose of private study, research, criticism or review, as permitted under the Copyright Act, 1956, no part of this publication may be reproduced, stored in a retrieval system, or transmitted in any form or by means, electronic, electrical, chemical, mechanical, optical, photocopying, recording or otherwise, without the prior permission of the copyright owner.

Enquiries should be sent to the publishers at the undermentioned address:

THE INSTITUTE OF BANKERS
10 Lombard Street
London EC3V 9AS

© The Institute of Bankers 1987 and L. S. Dyer F.I.B.

 British Library Cataloguing in Publication Data

Hutchinson, H. H.
    Interpretation of balance sheets. 6th ed.
    1. Financial statements
    I. Title   II. Dyer, L. S.

657.33'024332   HF5681.B2

ISBN 0 85297 176 1

Typeset in 10/11 Times Roman and printed by McCorquodale Confidential Print
Text printed on 115 gsm Motomatt Cartridge
Cover on 240 gsm

iv

INTERPRETATION OF BALANCE SHEETS

CONTENTS   Page No.

I

II

III

IV

V

VI

VII

VIII

FOREWORD

The first edition of *Interpretation of Balance Sheets* by the late H. H. Hutchinson FIB, a former Local Director of Barclays Bank, appeared in 1955. Since then it has become one of the most popular Institute publications.

The fifth and sixth editions were prepared by L. S. Dyer FIB formerly Managing Director of First National Finance Corporation. Although essential revision has been made, as much as possible of the original work and its character have been preserved.

The sixth edition still concentrates on the original theme that interpretation of past performance is an essential preliminary as an aid to the assessment of banking advances, although the value of forecasting is also touched upon.

The book has been brought into line with the style of the formats for balance sheets specified in the Companies Act 1985, the section on inflation has been brought up to date and new sections have been added on Statements of Source and Application of Funds and Accounting Ratios.

It is hoped that this book will help examination candidates to gain a basic knowledge of the interpretation of accounts and also be of assistance to lending bankers generally.

I

The practical approach

This book is concerned with the interpretation, not the preparation, of balance sheets, and its viewpoint is that of the lending banker, not the shareholder.

A notable disadvantage of balance sheets is that they record a position which existed on a certain date in the past, whereas what a banker who reads them chiefly wishes to know is the position which is likely to arise in the months or years to come. It is proposed here to discuss, therefore, not only methods of gathering factual information from a balance sheet, but also its value as a guide in the assessment of the future outlook for the business to which it relates.

In itself a balance sheet has little significance, and to base an interpretation exclusively upon an examination of its constituent items, without knowledge of the real. living, changing enterprise which it only imperfectly depicts, is to attempt the futile. There is not much to be gained, for example, by pondering over a figure for stock-in-trade if the nature of the business has not been ascertained. The stock might consist of ladies' hats or fresh fruit or pig iron or a thousand and one other things. If it were possible to devise a universal key which would interpret every balance sheet purely on the figures comprised in it, a book of tables in which a banker could find precise mathematical answers to all his questions and so might assess his risk by resolving a formula, banking life would be much simpler than it is today—and much less interesting. But no such universal key exists. Balance sheets are as varied as the human activities which they represent and cannot be usefully interpreted by means of a formula. Each one, to be properly understood, should be studied as an individual thing with its own merits and peculiarities. As Bernard Shaw said (in a different context), the golden rule is that there is no golden rule.

To know how an accountant sets about constructing a balance sheet is an advantage to a banker, but it is not his prime concern; after all, a doctor takes the temperature of his patients without needing to become an expert in the manufacture of thermometers. Conversely, the ability to break down a balance sheet into the original elements from which it has been composed is, by itself, not enough. Of greater value is the capacity to perceive the significance of the relationship which the balance sheet figures bear to each other and to judge the various items in the light of what is known of the business generally. For instance, a figure of £5,000 for book debts does not carry the same implications if trade creditors amount to £2,000 as it would carry if the trade creditors figure were £10,000. And there is not much point in comparing the two figures at all

1

without first finding out whether that particular business normally sells its goods for cash or on credit.

All this is the merest common sense; but then so much of the interpretation of balance sheets is mere common sense. The practical man, who knows how to run a business and how to make it pay, will usually form a much truer judgement of a balance sheet—assuming that he is able to read one at all—than can be obtained from the subtlest and most convincing exponent of pure theory.

Of necessity, in this book it would obviously be impossible to reproduce actual balance sheets and the circumstances of real banking problems for discussion in public. An attempt has been made to achieve verisimilitude, largely by repressing the temptation to prove or demonstrate theoretical points by the production of distorted examples which could not possibly arise in practice. However, to embark upon the concoction of balance sheets entails making a voyage over perilous and uncharted seas; and whether the attempt at realism has fallen overboard in the process must be left to the reader to judge.

The banking proposition
When a banker examines a balance sheet his prime and practical concern, generally speaking, is a banking proposition involving the lending of money. Very probably he has been asked to lend, or to continue lending, and he wishes to ascertain whether the lending may be considered safe and whether repayment within a reasonable time can be fairly foreseen. Until he knows what banking proposition is to be put before him there is little object in a close study of the balance sheet. He will not know how a bank advance is intended to fit into the general picture and he may waste a great deal of time. To lend £10,000 to a company owning assets which exceed its liabilities by £75,000 is a very different thing from lending the same company £100,000.

A balance sheet, then, may be looked upon for our present purpose as an aid to the assessment of a banking proposition. It is one source of some of the relevant information and although it is an important document it should be kept sternly in its place—which is to say in perspective.

Of course, there is more to know about a banking proposition than simply the amount of money required. The use to be made of the money is equally important. To lend a garage proprietor £20,000 to pay for new cars which he has already contracted for sale may be all very well; repayment should be almost automatic. To lend him the same amount of money so that he can maintain a larger stock of spares is something quite different; repayment will not come immediately from sale of the spares unless he reduces his total stocks to about their former level, which is the opposite of what he intends to do. If he asks for £20,000 to spend on altering his showrooms, still other considerations arise, as he could not repay by restoring his showrooms to their former state even if he wished to do so. Government policy has frequently compelled British banks to think critically about the use to be made of the money they are asked to lend; but we are not here concerned with government policy, and it is as a matter of sound practical banking that stress is laid upon the importance of ascertaining the purpose of an advance.

Asking the right questions
The main features of any banking proposition may be tabulated as follows:

(1) How much is required?
(2) What is to be done with the money?
(3) What are the plans for repayment?
(4) What will be the bank's position if the plans for repayment go wrong?

Points 1, 2 and 3 should be clearly grasped and in mind before examination of the balance sheet commences. Point 4 is a matter for the banker's personal assessment after he has examined the balance sheet and studied other relevant factors; he must also form his own opinion of the probability or otherwise of a failure of the plans for repayment as they are described by the borrowing customer.

With a firm grasp of what is proposed, the banker should turn his attention to obtaining a clear picture of the business which wishes to borrow the money. What is the nature of the business? Who owns it? Who runs it and with what success? Is it a large business or a small one in relation to the proposed borrowing? Is it stable and well-established? Are profits distributed or retained in the business? He should also consider how the banking proposition will fit into the picture which is taking shape in his mind and should form some idea of what the balance sheet position is likely to be after the bank has lent.

Much of the necessary information may already be available to him from his general knowledge of his customers; some he can obtain by examining the current account; some from a study of the balance sheet.

It may be helpful at this point to introduce an imaginary banking proposition together with the balance sheet of the company concerned.

CASE 1
Merlin Smew & Co. Ltd. is a private limited company engaged in the manufacture of fine worsted cloths. The business is old-established and

enjoys a good reputation in the trade; it has prospered under its present management.

The bank is asked to renew an unsecured overdraft limit of £45,000 for use in case of need. No substantial capital expenditure is contemplated and the money, if taken, will be used to finance trading. Little use has been made of the limit over the past twelve months and the account usually runs in good credit.

MERLIN SMEW AND CO. LTD.
Manufacturers of Fine Worsteds

ASSETS	£	LIABILITIES AND CAPITAL	£
Cash	28,378	Trade creditors	35,874
Local Authority Loans	28,000	Corporation tax	
Debtors	65,204 (f)	due in 4 months	8,090
Stock	114,813 (d)	Dividends including ACT ...	13,410
	236,395 (c)		57,374
		Corporation tax	
		due in 16 months	24,000
			81,374 (b)
Freehold property	75,271	Capital	140,000
Plant etc.	49,501	Reserves	49,100
		Profit and loss account	90,693 (h)
	£361,167 (a)		£361,167
Turnover (sales) for year	£565,000 (e)	Net profit for year	£36,000 (g)
		after tax	£24,000
		depreciation	£7,768
		directors' remuneration	£25,000

Turning now to the balance sheet of this company (as shown above) we observe, first of all, that it has been set out in a simplified form. The object of this is to give prominence to certain features and also to present the main facts and figures without a distracting mass of details and technicalities. Extracting the figures of a balance sheet in this way forms a useful preliminary to an assessment and, besides simplifying the general picture, prevents the overlooking of important items. The method of extraction adopted will be fully described later and it will suffice to remark here that the underlying principles are easy to grasp and may be mastered in a few minutes. Doubtless there are variations in detail between the methods of extraction practised in different banks, but the principles must be common to all.

A survey of the figures reveals the following points:

   (i) That at the date of the balance sheet the company had at its disposal assets of £361,167 (*a*). No intangible assets are included in this figure.

  (ii) That at the same date the company's debts totalled £81,374 (*b*) (including a sum of £24,000 for corporation tax not due for some months after the balance sheet date.)

 (iii) That the company's debts were covered more than four times by the assets. In other words, if the assets were worth together only one-quarter of their aggregate balance sheet value all the debts could still be paid in full.

  (iv) That the company had a surplus of £279,793 [(*a* minus (*b*)].

   (v) That out of total assets of £361,167 (*a*) no less than £236,395 (*c*) consisted either of cash or of items easily and regularly turned into cash (current assets). Thus, obviously, the company could pay all its creditors without having to sell its factory or plant; in fact the current assets are almost sufficient to cover all debts three times over [(*c*) compared with (*b*)]. In other words, the balance sheet shows a liquid position—and a strong one.

  (vi) That stocks on hand were not too high in relation to sales [(*d*) compared with (*e*) shows stocks on balance sheet date equivalent to about one-fifth of the total sold during the preceding year]. This is a manufacturing business and some time necessarily elapses between the purchase of yarn and the sale of cloth. If it were a purely merchanting business, selling goods in the same state as that in which it bought them, a higher rate of turnover of stocks might be expected, and would be evidenced by a stock figure which formed a smaller fraction of the figure for annual sales. Whether in any given case stocks are too high in relation to sales cannot be estimated without some knowledge of the course of business followed and where a banker is in doubt he should talk the matter over with his customer and use his own common sense and experience. For example, a whisky distillery advertising 'Not a drop sold till it's seven years old' will have a rate of stock turnover much slower than that of a fishmonger advertising 'Fresh fish daily'.

 (vii) That debtors were not unduly high in relation to sales [(*f*) compared with (*e*)] suggests that only one-ninth of the goods sold during the year had not been actually paid for on the date of the balance sheet. Here, again, knowledge of the course of business pursued by the customer is necessary for an intelligent view.

In this case sales would be on credit terms (few businesses, except retailers, sell much on cash terms nowadays) and a total of one-ninth outstanding suggests about 5–6 weeks' credit, varying, of course, if the trade has a heavy seasonal swing. At all events, if the outstanding one-ninth contains any debts which may prove to be bad the company has a surplus large enough to stand the loss. Bad debts are not probable, however, where a business has the successful profits record that this one can show.

(viii) That good profits were earned during the year (g) and have been made in the past (h). Note that profits earned and left in the business need not remain in the profit and loss account, but may appear as reserves, or may have been capitalised.

(ix) The only puzzle is why an overdraft limit of £45,000 is required at all. Perhaps, if several large contracts coincided, the account would become temporarily overdrawn. Possibly the directors are preparing for a large expansion in turnover.

A branch manager could soon elicit this information and in recommending renewal of the overdraft facilities might add the following remarks to the usual form of application to his head office. 'The directors ask for renewal for use in case of need in the ordinary course of trading. The overdraft will only be taken for short periods when large contracts coincide. The latest balance sheet is attached, showing a surplus of £280,000 over liabilities of £81,000 and a strong liquid position; and although we are unsecured there cannot be a risk. Good profits continue to be earned and a substantial proportion is left in the business'.

Head office ought to give an unqualified sanction.

The balance sheet summary

Before leaving the balance sheet of Merlin Smew & Co. Ltd., we will briefly examine the principles underlying the method of extraction demonstrated by the simplified layout on page 4. The distinctive feature of the extraction are the horizontal lines which divide both the liabilities and the assets into two groups as follows:

LIABILITIES (OR CLAIMS) SIDE

There are three groups. The final group consists of the owner's equity, and all other items are the true liabilities of the business including provisions for liabilities not yet due and including also any reserves which are in the nature of provisions. Whether a reserve should be shown among the true liabilities or in the final group depends on an assessment of the real purpose of the reserve. If the real purpose is to provide for some future liability or expenditure, or to offset some unexpected loss, the reserve should be included in the true liabilities and not with the owners' equity.

For instance, a reserve for repairs normally indicates future expenditure necessary to maintain the value of the fixed assets, and should go with the true liabilities.

The true liabilities are divided into two groups. In the second group are those liabilities which, at the balance sheet date, are not due for payment within twelve months. By the time that the balance sheet is received by the bank several months will have passed; these liabilities will by then be due that much earlier but, of course, some of the liabilities in the top group will also by then have been met.

In the top group are the current liabilities i.e. all those which are due for payment within twelve months of the balance sheet date. Where overdrafts are concerned, bankers are interested in the payments and receipts which are going through the banking account and these will consist, in the main, of those items shown in the current liabilities and current assets. That is why prominence is given to current liabilities and current assets by putting them at the top of the analysis.

In the group for the owners' equity are placed the capital, the remaining reserves and the balance of profit and loss account if in credit. If profit and loss account is 'in the red', i.e., in debit, it will appear among the intangible assets on the other side of the extraction of the balance sheet, and, together with other intangible assets, should be deducted from the total of capital and reserves in order to arrive at the true surplus, or net worth, of the business as disclosed in the balance sheet.

ASSETS SIDE

The line divides the quick or current assets from the fixed, long-term, intangible or doubtful assets. *Above the line* is the place for the assets relating to the day-to-day trading. For an ordinary commercial or industrial business they will consist of cash; debtors; stock; work-in-progress. With these should be included any *marketable* (i.e., listed) investments not held as long term investments and also any temporary deposits of cash, such as local authority deposits, building society deposits etc.

Items to be placed below the line include listed investments which are held for the long term, non-listed investments, investments in and amounts due by subsidiary or associated companies; and loans (now very restricted) to directors. Prepayments also are usually placed below the line, but the amount is commonly quite small and so the point is not very important.

Below the line are set out such items as land and buildings, plant, motor lorries, etc.; the intangibles such as goodwill, patent rights and kindred items; a debit balance on profit and loss account; and any other assets which either do not relate to the day-to-day trading or are in any way dubious. Amounts owing by the directors or by associated companies go

7

below the line not because they are considered bad, but because payment is frequently a matter of arrangement between the parties and may not arise naturally in the ordinary course of business.

The extraction of a balance sheet is not a complex matter, but it calls for some judgement and also for some consistency of practice if the results are to be clear and simple to grasp. Each person should ascertain and follow the practice of his own bank, but it is better to do so with understanding than by rule of thumb.

At the foot of the extraction we show certain figures taken not from the balance sheet, but from the usual accompanying accounts. Below the assets column appears the total of sales for the year, which may be obtained from the trading account. Below the liabilities column appears the net profit figure after allowing for tax and for the other items shown. The net profit (or loss) figure should always be compared with the increase (or decrease) in the surplus since the date of the last balance sheet and any difference accounted for. Any exceptional features, such as the introduction of fresh capital, the recovery or writing back of tax, profits or losses on sale of capital items, should be specially noted; and a prominent comment should be added if the company is factoring or discounting its book debts (see p. 25 on factoring).

It must be appreciated, however, that while this short analysis enables a quick view to be taken, a more detailed method must be employed for complicated propositions and involved audited figures. Also, when a banker has several years of balance sheets available, he is able to extract the figures from each balance sheet in columnar form in order to compare the figures year by year. This is naturally a more satisfactory way and an example will be shown later; for the time being we will use the short analysis method to demonstrate the important features of a single year's figures.

CASE 2

It was easy to see from the balance sheet of Merlin Smew & Co. Ltd., that the proposed limit involved no risk. Let us now look at the affairs of a company in different circumstances.

Dipper Dunlin & Co. Ltd. are general merchants and shippers, buying a miscellaneous range of goods and selling them at home and abroad wherever they find a suitable market. Some of their special lines are manufactured for them under contract. The account is an old one, going back over fifty years. The managing director is the son of the original founder, and there is another director who joined the board when the company absorbed another business some years ago. Both directors are respected and trustworthy.

There is an overdraft limit of £15,000 originally granted for trading purposes and this is unsecured except for the joint and several guarantee of the directors. Formerly the account fluctuated well and credit balances were often seen, but over the past year there has been a marked change, fluctuations have grown progressively less, the overdraft now rarely falling below £12,000, and there have been some excesses.

The new balance sheet accompanies a request for continuance of the limit. This is shown in a simplified form below.

DIPPER DUNLIN & CO. LTD.
General Merchants and Shippers

	£	£	£
Fixed assets			
Furniture, Motors etc.			25,902
Trade Investments			4,066
Shares in Subsidiary Companies			2,300
Patents and Licences			15,466
Goodwill			4,998
			52,732
Current assets			
Cash	376		
Debtors	37,972		
Stock	61,732	100,080	
Less current liabilities			
Trade Creditors	75,788		
Bank	14,626	90,414	9,666
			62,398
Less loan creditors			27,412
			£34,986
Represented by shareholders' funds			
Capital		32,000	
Reserves		804	
Profit and Loss Account		2,182	£34,986

It will be seen that this balance sheet is in columnar form which is now commonly used. Companies now have to use the formats set out in the Companies Act 1985 and most of them are using the columnar form (known as format 1). Balance sheets are often shown with few figures appearing but with all the details in notes attached. A banker will have to examine the notes thoroughly in order to understand the figures and then extract those he requires; the principles for extraction of a balance sheet summary still apply. Following these principles and obtaining relative information from the profit and loss account, the summary will be written as follows;

DIPPER DUNLIN AND CO. LTD.

General Merchants and Shippers

ASSETS	£	LIABILITIES AND CAPITAL	£
Cash	376	Trade Creditors	75,788
Debtors	37,972	Bank	14,626
Stock	61,732		
	100,080		90,414
		Loan Creditors	27,412
			117,826
Furniture, Motors etc.	25,902	Capital	32,000
Trade investments	4,066	Reserves	804
Shares in subsidiaries	2,300	Profit and loss account	2,182
Patents and licences	15,466		
Goodwill	4,998		
	£152,812		£152,812
Sales (Year)	£356,546	Loss (Year)	£764
		after	
		tax	nil
		depreciation	636
		directors' remuneration ...	£24,000

The figures show liabilities of £117,826 and total assets of £152,812, giving a nominal surplus of about £35,000. However. the assets include goodwill, £4,998, and patents and licences, £15,466, and after deduction of these intangibles the surplus shrinks to less than £15,000. Even this is open to question as the assets also contain trade investments, £4,066 (a new item since the last balance sheet) and shares in subsidiary companies shown at £2,300. The trade investments may or may not be marketable. The shares in subsidiary companies may be worth many thousands of pounds or nothing at all; without a sight of the balance sheets of the companies concerned it would be unwise to hazard a guess. If both these items were bad the surplus would fall below £9,000.

The liquid position is even bleaker as if we compare the current assets with the true liabilities there is a deficit of £17,746 below £117,826. If the loans were not long term ones the company would soon be faced with the problem of their repayment. If they were long term the position would be a little better as the net current assets show a surplus of £9,666 but this is not a great sum when creditors are also twice as much as debtors and the stock accounts for 60% of the current assets. Profits are a minus quantity after the directors' remuneration of £24,000.

It should be noted that under the Companies Act 1985 patents, licences and trade marks can only be included in the assets if they were acquired for valuable consideration and are not required to be shown under goodwill, or if they are created by the company itself. Goodwill can only be included to the extent that it is acquired for valuable consideration. Goodwill has to be written off over its useful economic life which must be disclosed in the accounts. Statement of Standard Accounting Practice 22 (SSAP 22) recommends that goodwill should be written off to reserves and not carried in the balance sheet. If it is carried in the balance sheet it will, of course, be written off in the profit and loss account over a period. There are, therefore, two treatments for writing off goodwill. When it is carried in the balance sheet it will cause the accountancy profits to be lower in future years than would be the case when it is written off straight away to reserves.

Faced with these figures and bearing in mind the serious worsening of the run of the account, a branch manager might well feel concerned. Part of the heavier overdraft will have arisen as a result of the investment of £4,066, but more than that is needed to account for a swing over from an in-and-out overdraft to a solid lending of £12–15,000. Capital expenditure of £8–10,000 could account for the remainder of the change and whether this is, in fact, the cause may be ascertained by comparing the total of fixed assets in the new balance sheet with that in the previous one. If there has been no substantial capital expenditure the probability is that amongst the goods purchased during the year some £8–10,000-worth have proved unsaleable or at least have not yet found a buyer. The stock figure of £61,732 must accordingly be suspect. Other possible explanations are that debtors are taking longer to pay or that one big debt has been outstanding for a long time, or that creditors have been insisting upon prompter settlement; there may be a combination of these causes. A detailed comparison of the new balance sheet with the previous one will help in elucidating the problem, but in the end the best plan in such cases is to ask the customer for an explanation and then to check what he says by reference to the balance sheet figures.

The poor results for the year also throw doubt upon the stock figure. In a business like this stocks which have been well-bought and are turning over should naturally produce good profits.

If the company has, indeed, purchased £10,000 of goods which are unsaleable a serious situation may arise. We have seen that the surplus (or net worth) of the business may be only £9,000. A loss of £10,000 would transform that surplus into a deficit and the company might be forced into liquidation. This, in its turn, would create further losses since on a forced sale the remaining good stocks could not be relied upon to fetch more than 50 per cent. or so of their balance sheet valuation—say, £30,000 instead of £61,732. They might not realize more than £10,000 or £15,000. Thus, the first loss of £10,000 on the bad stock might well lead to an equivalent or greater loss on a forced sale of the good stock. Any furniture and fittings would also sell very badly in a liquidation.

Of course, there is no need to suppose that a business is faced with ruin if it is left with unsold stock or, indeed, if it incurs an outright loss. The question is: has the business sufficient resources of its own to meet the loss—and, in particular, has it sufficient liquid resources? If a company loses money, it loses first the profits and reserves accumulated in the past, then its share capital and only after these are gone is the money of creditors imperilled. The whole stake of the shareholders in the business—capital, reserves and undistributed profits—has to be lost before the creditors lose a penny piece. Thus the surplus (net worth) forms a margin or buffer between the creditors and disaster.

For that reason it is important to ensure that an unsecured lending by a bank is not too great in relation to the surplus in the business: that the margin of safety is adequate. The adequacy of the surplus in relation to the total liabilities should also be watched, since in the last resort it is a margin of protection for all creditors.

Watch also the current assets in relation to the current liabilities. If a company trades profitably the net current assets will rise unless all the profits are used for purchase of fixed assets or for dividends. This increase in net current assets gives comfort to a bank for its lending. If losses are made, the net current assets will fall and a company may then have to resort to raising funds on its fixed assets or selling them in order to keep faith with its obligations to its bankers and creditors.

When lending on overdraft it is the trading results which matter and these are reflected in the net current assets.

What is a proper ratio between the surplus, the net current assets and an unsecured bank lending depends very much on the circumstances of each individual case. It would be rash to lend without security the equivalent of half the surplus in a business if the surplus were all sunk in fixed assets or if there were a bad profit record or if unsold stock were too high. On the other hand, certain types of borrowers frequently borrow much more than their surplus. Corn merchants, for example, may overdraw heavily at the peak of their season when they are buying grain to fill firm orders.

Returning now to the affairs of Dipper Dunlin & Co. Ltd., let us suppose that the branch manager ascertains by enquiry that the 'trade investments' of £4,066 represents an interest-bearing loan obtained in lieu of an unsatisfactory book debt, and that the shares in subsidiary companies are valueless. The directors admit that they have paid £10,000 for stocks which have proved difficult to sell, but they still hope to bring off a satisfactory deal.

What the branch manager then decides to recommend will depend largely on the value which he is able to attach to the directors' guarantee that is held. If it is safely worth £15,000 there cannot be any risk; if it is of little real value some provision against ultimate loss may be advisable. He would, in the normal course, already know something of the position of the guarantors.

It would not be much use demanding a debenture, because of the publicity involved, which, in the circumstances of this company, would promptly bring pressure from creditors and, unless the limit were increased so that they could be paid, liquidation might supervene before the debenture would have had time to 'harden'.

Balance sheet check-list

The main value of a study of a balance sheet is the help it gives towards obtaining a clear idea of the business to which it relates. In studying a balance sheet:

The *nature of the business* is an important consideration because it indicates what the stock consists of and suggests how rapid a turnover ought to be expected.

The *purpose of the proposed advance* is an important consideration because it indicates whether the advance will be self-liquidating, helps to show whether it should be short-term, fluctuating, or solid and enables one to estimate whether the results of the lending will be an impairment of the liquidity of the business.

The *surplus* (net worth) shown in the balance sheet is important because it represents a margin or buffer which stands between the creditors (including the bank) and disaster. It is the stake which the proprietors have in the business and would all have to be lost before creditors could suffer.

The *liquid position* is important because it indicates whether liabilities could be met without recourse to the fixed assets of the business. To ensure this, there should be a margin of liquidity (liquid surplus) of adequate size in relation to the true liabilities.

The relationship of *stock to annual sales* is important because it may point to over-stocking or unsaleable stock.

The relationship of *debtors to annual sales* is important as a rough guide to the average period of credit granted.

The *profits record* is important because if adequate and steady profits have been earned they support faith in the balance sheet value of the current assets and in the business capabilities of the management. Profits which have been left to accumulate in the business indicate growth and prudent control.

II

Working capital

The day-to-day running of a business requires finance over and above that which is necessary for purchase of fixed assets, and the volume of work or trading which can safely be undertaken depends not only upon the equipment and labour which the business controls but also upon the finance which is available. Debtors, stock and work-in-progress have to be carried all the time, and whilst the amount of each of these and the aggregate total of all of them may fluctuate very considerably, there must always be a matching aggregate total of finance upon which they can ride. This finance is provided either from the proprietors' stake in the business (capital, reserves and undistributed profits) or by borrowing (loan creditors, bank overdrafts, mortgages, etc.) or by obtaining credit for goods and services employed. In addition, money earmarked to meet liabilities not yet due, taxation for example, may be used meanwhile to finance current trading. And since none of these sources provides unlimited money or credit it follows that there is an upper limit upon the total of current assets which may be carried.

The proprietors' stake in an ordinary business, then, ought to be sufficient to cover, in the first place, the amount sunk in fixed assets and intangibles plus any amounts lent to directors or invested in other businesses; there should then be a further sum available to finance trading (i.e., available as working capital). To ascertain from a balance sheet how much working capital there is, it is necessary merely to subtract the current liabilities from the current assets i.e., in our method of extraction this is the total of liabilities in the top group from the total of assets in the top group.

Here is a simplified balance sheet by way of illustration.

AORNON LTD.

	£
Assets	
Land and Buildings	25,000
Plant, etc.	11,450
Debtors	8,500
Stock	5,790
Work in Progress	4,625
	55,365

Less liabilities	£	
Trade Creditors	6,000	
Loan Creditors	1,250	
Bank	1,175	
Corporation Tax— 5 months	740	
17 months	1,520	10,685
		£44,680

Shareholders' funds	
Capital	26,500
Reserves	14,600
Profit and Loss Account	3,580
	£44,680

These figures are summarized according to our principles of extraction as follows:

AORNON LTD.

	£		£
Debtors	8,500	Trade creditors	6,000
Stock	5,790	Bank	1,175
Work in progress	4,625	Corporation tax 5 months	740
	18,915		7,915
		Loan Creditors	1,250
		Corporation tax 17 months	1,520
			10,685
Land and buildings	25,000	Capital	26,500
Plant etc.	11,450	Reserves	14,699 } (a)
		Profit and loss account	3,580
	£55,365		£55,365

The business has a surplus of £44,680 (*a*) of which £36,450 is sunk in premises and plant and the working capital is £11,000 (£18,915 minus £7,915).

Current assets totalling £18,915 were being carried at the balance sheet date and these were being financed from the following sources:

	£
Working capital	11,000
Bank	1,175
Credit obtained for goods, etc. employed	6,000
Unpaid tax—due in 5 months	740
	£18,915

The total of current assets naturally fluctuates from day-to-day, with a corresponding fluctuation on the other side of the balance sheet. There will also be changes in the composition of the figures for current assets and current liabilities. Thus a payment of £500 for wages would increase both work-in-progress and the bank overdraft; payment by a debtor of an amount of £750 would decrease both debtors and the bank overdraft; purchase of raw materials for £600 would increase trade creditors and stock; payment of £500 on account of taxation would decrease the tax liability and increase the bank overdraft. But the two sides could not get out of line. It would not be possible, for example, to acquire a net £10,000 more stock *and* increase the total of current assets by that figure without a corresponding increase on the liabilities side. The business would of necessity either owe for the stock or pay for it, and in the latter event the money paid would have to be provided either from earnings or as additional share capital or by a lender.

Effect of increased turnover
In all businesses, if the volume of trading and the course of business remain steady, the limits within which the total of current assets will fluctuate are fairly well defined and so long as the maximum figure for current assets can be matched without overstretching the finance available the trading remains four-square and firm. But suppose that the directors decide—or are tempted—to undertake twice as much business, what will be the effect on the structure of the trading finance? Doubling the turnover, if the same period of credit is still allowed to purchasers, will double the average amount owing by debtors and probably the peak amount also. Doubling the output of the factory will perhaps double the amount of work in progress. Stocks of raw materials and of finished goods will also show an increase. Thus the total of current assets will certainly increase

17

very sharply and may well double as the turnover doubles. What about finance? Unless more cash capital is introduced, the amount of working capital available will remain as it was, rising gradually if profits are earned. Trade creditors will increase, since more raw materials will be purchased, probably to about double the former figure if the company has a good record, but this will not fill the whole gap. Let us look again at the trading figures in the balance sheet of Aornon Ltd.

If trading doubles, the current assets of Aornon Ltd. may rise to about £38,000—perhaps more at peak periods. How can this be carried?

	£
Working capital (as before	11,000
Credit obtainable (double)	12,000
Unpaid tax	740
	23,740
Balance to be raised by borrowing	14,260
	£38,000

It will be seen, therefore, that if no additional capital is put into this business a very large increase in borrowing would become necessary if turnover were doubled (possibly £14,260 compared with £1,175). In addition, a larger margin of cash would have to be available for peak periods or for emergencies. If the company asked its bank for the additional money, an overdraft limit, of say, £15,000 would be needed instead of about £1,500.

By a similar calculation it will be found that redoubling the turnover might necessitate an overdraft limit of as much as £40–50,000.

Perhaps it should be stressed here that doubling the turnover does not automatically entail doubling the current assets, trebling the turnover trebling the current assets and so on. Any large increase in turnover leads to an increase in current assets but the extent of the increase is a matter for calculation and enquiry.

Overtrading

Overtrading, that is to say undertaking more business than can be conveniently supported by the finance available, has ruined many good little businesses and not a few large ones. It is difficult for an enterprising young manufacturer to understand that there is anything imprudent in accepting profitable orders; moreover he knows that if he declines them he may not get similar chances in future. If he takes on more work than he ought there follows inevitably a distortion of his trading position, and this will eventually be reflected in his balance sheet. In order to have cash for wages he postpones paying his trade creditors; when the trade creditors press he starts trying to collect his book debts early, or pays the creditors small amounts on account, or gives out post-dated cheques, or persuades the bank to give him a temporary excess overdraft on the strength of money expected in from debtors. Eventually, in a bad case, he may reach a point where he has a stock of partly-manufactured goods which cannot be completed because he can neither pay cash for some essential components or materials, nor obtain them on credit. Or he may have to discharge labour in order to reduce his wages bill; then production will fall behind and ready cash will be further off than ever. His skilled workmen will leave him for more reliable employment.

An example can be quoted of a case where a whole consignment of expensive machinery was held up for two months for lack of paint to finish it off. The workmen in the factory were highly skilled, and rather than allow the team to disperse, the manufacturer kept them employed on such parts of the job in his overflowing order book as could be turned out from the materials which he had in store. Meanwhile every penny which he could raise, from his bank and elsewhere, went in wages and the factory became cluttered up with half-finished jobs; nothing could be completed and so nothing could be delivered and turned into money.

However, there are degrees of overtrading and it should not be supposed that every business which overtrades is doomed. Indeed some very fine and substantial businesses have passed through periods of what a purist would call overtrading. Most bank managers, particularly in the London area, have customers who seriously overtrade but yet survive. The acrobatic feats of finance by which some of them conduct their businesses without visible means of support have to be seen to be believed.

CASE 3

The two balance sheets which now follow reveal a sharp contrast in the relationship of the various trading figures. The first is the balance sheet of a well-managed company of timber merchants and shows substantial working capital. Overdraft facilities of £50,000 are available without security; the account swings comfortably and, except at the seasonal peaks, borrowing is usually well below the limit.

PRATINCOLE PLOVER AND CO. LTD.

Timber Merchants

	£		£
Debtors	38,060	Creditors	16,973
Stock	37,950	Bank	6,960
		Corporation tax—2 months ...	5,424
		Bonus to directors	375
		Dividends plus ACT	3,700
	76,010		33,432
		Deferred tax	6,450
			39,882
Freeholds	39,805	Capital	80,000
Plant and machinery	18,875	Reserves	28,000
Shares in subsidiaries	13,839	Profit and loss account	3,260
Trade investments	1,927		
Loans	686		
	£151,142		£151,142
Sales	£430,000		

Of the company's surplus of £111,260, fixed assets and other 'below-the-line' items absorb £75,132, the working capital is £42,578.

The directors of the business, therefore, have to say to themselves:

'We must not allow our aggregate current assets (debtors and stock in this case) to run up to a figure which is higher than the total of the following items, plus any profits earned as we go along'.

	£
Working capital	42,578
Banking facilities	50,000
One month's creditors, say	30,000
	£122,578

'We will call it £110,000 to be on the safe side and to leave a margin of overdraft for cash requirements. If our total stock and debtors looks likely to rise above that figure we must start drawing in our horns, unless we can get more overdraft from the bank. Furthermore, if we decide to spend substantial sums on fixed assets or to buy more trade investments we must remember that by so doing we are consuming some of our working capital and are therefore reducing to that extent the total of current assets which we are able to carry.'

CASE 4

The balance sheet of the second company discloses a very different state of affairs. Godwit & Goldfinch Ltd. is a small company of clothing manufacturers managed by two directors, who are capable, energetic, go-ahead young men with good knowledge and experience of the trade. They have no means outside this business and one or two other small companies in ancillary trades. The account was transferred from another bank about six months ago and has been active with a substantial turnover; it swings into good credit month by month but gives a little trouble about the time of the monthly settlement.

An application is made for an unsecured overdraft limit of £12,000 to finance a contract from first-class buyers for a quantity of raincoats. The contract is for £50,000 and repayment of the overdraft is promised within four months.

GODWIT AND GOLDFINCH LTD.

Clothing Manufacturers

	£		£
Cash	11,946	Trade Creditors	55,065
Trade Debtors	16,613	Loans by Directors	5,318
Stock and Work in Progress ..	23,034		
	51,593		60,383
Plant machinery and motors ..	8,540	Capital	2,500
Prepayments	640	Profit and loss account	267
Goodwill	2,377		
			£63,150
	£63,150		
		Stock purchases	£148,400
Sales	£260,000	Profit (year)	4,257
		after	
		tax	nil
		depreciation	1,240
		directors' remuneration ...	12,000
		goodwill written off	500

Nominally there is a surplus in this business of £2,767 but it shrinks to £400 after deduction of the goodwill, and, apart from this, the only item which could be quasi-capital is the directors' loans amounting to £5,318. Loan capital is a very different thing from share capital but at least the directors have some money in the business, and it might be possible to have the loans postponed to the bank. However, even if we regard the directors' loans as capital, the whole surplus—and nearly £3,000 more—is sunk in plant, machinery and motors. Thus there is a deficit of working capital, reflected in the fact that the balance sheet is unliquid to the extent of nearly £9,000, or nearly £3,500 if the directors' loans are regarded as capital. In other words, the whole of the finance which carries the current assets, plus £3,500 more, has been found by the trade creditors. Do not be deceived by the fact that on the balance sheet date there was £11,946 cash in hand and at the bank; the money clearly belongs to the creditors in every moral sense and it is only through their forbearance that the company's banking account shows a substantial, though temporary, credit balance. Looking at the trade creditors figure of £55,000 in relation to a business with a capital of £5,700, nearly all on loan, and a turnover of £260,000, one is tempted to remark that the forbearance of its creditors is this company's principal asset.

Part of the figure for trade creditors will represent accrued expenses, but if there is £50,000 owing for materials the period of credit which the company is taking is far above normal. Stock purchases for the whole year were only £148,400. The liability to trade creditors needs probing—the balance sheet tells us no more about it than that it is high—and in particular the bank manager should enquire who are the principal creditors and whether they have any family connection with this company.

Profits were made in the year covered by the accounts but it will be seen that the profit and loss balance is only £267 after bringing in net profits of £4,257; the previous balance sheet must therefore have shown the profit and loss account on the wrong side to the tune of £3,990, evidence that substantial losses had been incurred in past trading.

The strength of the proposal is the contract; the buyers are undoubted for £50,000 and the raincoats are to be completed and delivered within four months. The contract price provides an ample profit margin and the directors press strongly for the bank's support. They offer personal guarantees and postponement of their own loans but refuse a debenture on the plea that this would bring the company's creditors about their ears.

Quite probably, if the bank lent the £12,000 all would go well; but is the risk worth taking? The company has little resources to weather any storm and might be in trouble if there were a power-cut or a strike or a breakdown of machinery and the raincoats were not completed by the contracted date. Even the most undoubted of buyers cannot be expected to accept delivery of goods which come to him too late and have missed their market. Moreover the company is very vulnerable to its creditors, who could bring it down at any moment and who might, after all, be compelled to call for their money by circumstances outside their own control. The company has incurred losses in the past, possibly owing to bad costing or faulty workmanship, and, although the company has survived so far, £12,000 would be a rash lending without tangible security.

This is a case of gross overtrading, and evidence of it is in the distortion of the trading structure, of the relationship between current assets and current liabilities. Not only is there no liquid surplus but also creditors have been forced up to a figure far exceeding debtors. Naturally, if a profitable business both takes and allows the same period of credit, the debtors figure should exceed the trade creditors figure as a consequence of the sale of goods for more than has been expended on them. This is not to be regarded as a rule for general application but in this particular case the disparity is so great, even after reducing the creditors figure by the amount of cash in hand, and allowing for a possibility that at the date of the balance sheet some of the work in progress may have been at the point of completion and delivery, as to give rise to an immediate suspicion of overtrading.

Another indication that the business is over-extended may be seen in the fact that it owes amounts so vastly in excess of the stake of the proprietors.

Increase of fixed assets

Before leaving the subject of overtrading there are two further important points to mention. The first is the interrelation between overtrading and expenditure on fixed assets. Primarily, overtrading is a matter affecting the trading figures of a business: the current assets and current liabilities. In practice, when a business embarks upon a substantially increased volume of work, the directors generally find that they need to increase the fixed assets. To cope with the enlarged order-book more plant and machinery may be needed, more delivery vans, perhaps an extension of the factory. Unless fresh capital is introduced, the purchase of additional fixed assets will entail the absorption for that purpose of a greater part than before of the proprietor's stake in the business (the surplus) with a corresponding reduction of working capital. Thus, just when more finance is needed to carry the increasing turnover, one part of the finance available becomes lessened. Where resources are ample this does not matter in the least, but where an enlarged turnover is itself going to expose the business to the risk of overtrading, the purchase of more fixed assets, by depleting the working capital, creates an additional strain. Similarly, where the existing level of trading is already calling upon the financial resources available to a business, the sinking of a substantial sum in additional fixed assets may create an overtrading position by reducing working capital below the safety figure, even though there is no increase in turnover. In fact an unwise purchase of fixed assets may entail an enforced reduction of turnover and so prevent the new acquisitions from earning their keep.

Stock and debtors

The other important point is the relationship between overtrading and liquidity, using the term 'liquidity' in its stricter sense to denote having cash ready to meet cash calls. When we say that a balance sheet is liquid we may mean no more that that it shows an excess of current assets over current liabilities, but a business which is liquid in that sense may still be short of the wherewithal to pay the wages or the rate collector or a trade creditor. Book debts and stock are current assets, but it has been remarked elsewhere that cheques cannot be drawn on book debts; neither will workmen accept their wages in stock. A business must always have available to it a margin of cash or of unused overdraft facilities. Without cash on the spot and when it is required, the fact that trading is profitable will be cold comfort. Overtrading, as we have seen, imposes a strain upon all the finances of a business, not least upon the banking account, and where too great a part of the resources is tied up in stock and book debts there will be constant pressure on the overdraft limit and constant difficulty in finding ready money to meet wages and to pay accounts as they fall due. The practical question for a banker is how to recognize or detect serious overtrading by examination of a balance sheet; unfortunately there is no brief practical answer. So much, as always, depends upon the nature of the business, the experience and skill of those who are running it, and the terms of credit which it is customary to obtain and to allow in the particular trade.

Warning signs

Overtrading should always be suspected, however, in the following circumstances:

(i) Where a business is obtaining longer credit and/or allowing shorter credit *than is customary* in that particular trade. Test for this by comparing creditors with purchases, and debtors with sales and by enquiry of the directors as to their terms of business.

(ii) Where a business is obtaining longer credit and/or allowing shorter credit *than it used to do*. Test by comparing balance sheets for three successive years. If creditors are steadily rising and debtors are falling or static, or if the ratio between the two is steadily deteriorating, ask for an explanation.

(iii) Where the current liabilities of a business are much in excess of the surplus, particularly where such excess cannot be explained by seasonal peaks in the trade and where it shows a substantially rising tendency over three successive years.

(iv) Where the banking account reveals signs of hand-to-mouth finance: for example, a rising average overdraft coupled with a smaller swing and the development of a 'hard core'; weekly excesses for wages and pressure on the limit generally (assuming that the limit is not unduly small!); failure to cover cheques until they are presented; payments to suppliers in round amounts (too much importance should not be attached to this unless other signs are present); issuing of post-dated cheques.

Factoring

Over recent years there has been a considerable development in the 'factoring' of book debts; factoring is one of the financial services now offered by many banks through their associated companies.

Basically, factoring need involve no more than an arrangement with a specialist company for supervising, insuring and collecting book debts. Approved book debts are assigned, at the invoice stage, to the factoring company, which collects the money in due course and pays it over to the trading company approximately when received.

Owing to the expense of factoring, it is not usually worth while unless annual sales run up to £100,000 or more, and individual debts are well into four figures.

It is common for the trading company to be allowed to borrow from the factoring company before the book debts fall due; and such borrowings may be with or without recourse should the book debts prove bad. Interest is charged in addition to the usual factoring charges.

Factoring companies will also, in suitable cases, provide loans against book debts which are not subject to a factoring arrangement, and which the trading company itself will collect. This is called invoice discounting.

The effects of arrangements of these types on a trading company's balance sheet are as follows:

(i) Pure factoring has no visible effect on the balance sheet itself; the total of book debts remains the same, although the factoring company has undertaken responsibility for them. Factoring charges will appear in the profit and loss account accompanying the balance sheet.

(ii) Where the trading company borrows against factored debts *without recourse,* the primary effect on the balance sheet is analogous to that of a sudden increase in the proportion of cash sales. Debtors, as shown in the balance sheet, fall in amount, and there is a resultant increase in other assets or a decrease in liabilities, or both. Factoring charges, and interest, will appear in the profit and loss account.

25

(iii) Where such a borrowing is *with recourse,* or where there is borrowing by way of invoice discounting, the effect on the balance sheet *figure* is the same as (ii) above, but there will be a separate *note* on the balance sheet showing the amount of the contingent liability under the recourse agreement. Interest and other charges will appear in the profit and loss account.

In none of these cases is a charge registered against a borrowing company. The transactions are treated, technically, as purchase-and-sale transactions, not borrowings; and the factoring company becomes the owner of the book debts which it has bought from the trading company. Where a bank holds a debenture giving a floating charge on the book debts of a company, any such transactions would necessitate an agreement between the bank and the factoring company (itself possibly part of the same banking group).

Factoring is growing, and every banker dealing with trading or commercial advances should be alert to the possibilities. Where a company has sold or mortgaged its book debts, there is obviously less scope for ordinary bank lending, particularly by way of unsecured overdraft.

Deferred liabilities

Now just a brief word on the rather important topic of deferred liabilities. Corporation tax is the example most frequently seen.

Generally speaking, in the case of companies formed since 6 April 1965, corporation tax is assessed on the profits of their own trading year, and becomes payable nine months after that trading year has ended.

For companies formed before 6 April 1965 (and for some later companies which are regarded as continuations of earlier companies), the profits of their *trading* year are regarded as the taxable basis for the succeeding *fiscal* year (i.e. the year to 31 March annually) and corporation tax is payable on 1 January next following.

Thus there is a minimum time-lag of nine months, for both types of company, between the end of the trading year in which profits are earned and the due date for payment of corporation tax thereon. For the older companies there may be a longer time-lag, up to a maximum of 21 months.

By the due date for payment, if business is satisfactory, further profits will have been earned and a further sum of future corporation tax will have accumulated in the hands of the company. This process may continue for years and the result may be that the company has in use as working capital for all that time a substantial revolving sum over and above the true working capital. There is nothing wrong in this but it does explain why a banking account sometimes runs so much more easily than the extract of the balance sheet suggests that it ought.

A rather similar position arises where loan moneys or mortgage moneys have been put into the business for a fixed or minimum term. The liquid position as indicated by the extract of the balance sheet will be much less favourable than the directors will find it to be in practice. For the duration of the loan or mortgage they are able to use the money which has been lent as though it were part of the capital of the business.

In estimating the future requirements of a company by way of overdraft it is important to know when tax or loans will have to be cleared and unless the due date is shown in the balance sheet the bank manager should enquire of the directors or of the company's accountants.

Taxation

The effect of taxation on the activities of companies is so important that all but the smallest companies have to take advice from their auditors on this subject. The auditors themselves employ specialists. The subject is complicated and becoming more so as each year additional legislation has to be studied. This is not the place to give even a partial resumé of tax legislation but for a full understanding of accounts a banker must acquire knowledge of taxation as it affects business enterprises.

One of the difficulties associated with the understanding of taxation is that the tax to be paid is assessed on an amount of profits different from that shown in accounts. Company accounts are prepared on recognised accounting principles but the calculation of taxable profits is prepared according to the specific requirements of legislation. The result is that two different figures for profits emerge. Additionally, although an amount may be shown in a Profit and Loss account as tax, it is still not the amount that will be paid to the tax authorities on the due date for payment of tax for that particular year. This is because the tax shown in the Profit and Loss account is an amalgam of tax to be paid on the due date plus deferred taxation. The amount shown in the Profit and Loss account is split when appearing in the balance sheet, a part appearing as tax payable on the due date for tax for that particular year and the remainder being added to the deferred taxation account.

However, there can be inter-company transactions in a Group or various set-offs can apply which, when the time comes, make the amount paid to the tax authorities different from that shown in the accounts. A banker can, of course, take a cautious view and assume for his purpose that the amount of tax shown as due will in fact be paid at the correct time. There are many occasions, however, when more accurate information is necessary and the only way to obtain this is to ask the company concerned.

27

Deferred taxation

Considerable debate and confusion has arisen over the accountancy treatment of deferred taxation. Fortunately, from 1 January 1979, this was resolved by the introduction of Statement of Standard Accounting Practice No. 15 (SSAP 15): *Accounting for Deferred Taxation*. Balance sheets prepared after this date will, in numerous cases, have a different treatment from those prepared previously.

Before 1 January 1979 the amount of the deferred taxation account shown in many balance sheets comprised the full amount of the deferred taxation liability, whether or not such amount was ever likely to be paid in tax. This has now changed and the amount shown in balance sheets since 1 January 1979 is the amount which the directors consider to be the sum that will have to be paid in tax in the foreseeable future (say within three years).

The difference between the amounts to be paid in tax in the foreseeable future and the full liability for deferred taxation is made up, to a large extent, of amounts which it is assumed will be offset by taxation allowances receivable in subsequent years.

For example, amounts for capital allowances and depreciation are different. It is normal practice to debit to profit and loss accounts amounts for depreciation of plant and machinery, but for calculating taxable profits these items are eliminated. Instead, capital allowances are deducted from profits (or added to losses) and these allowances are determined by the Finance Acts. For example, in the past, capital allowances have been as much as 100 per cent. of the purchase price of depreciable assets. In these circumstances, capital allowances have been much greater than the amounts of depreciation, and the taxable profits have been reduced in the initial year in which capital allowances were claimed. In subsequent years there would be no further capital allowances to be claimed for the same items and the taxable profits would be relatively higher. Capital allowances can, of course, vary according to Government policy but the principle remains. To provide for this timing difference of tax payable in subsequent years an adjusting entry is passed to the deferred taxation account. However, such timing differences are in many cases of a recurring nature; allowances on additional capital expenditure in future years can equal or exceed the taxation which would otherwise have been payable in consequence of the reversal of the original timing difference.

There is little point in showing a deferred taxation liability for a timing difference on capital allowances if a company replaces or buys depreciable assets annually of a sufficient amount to offset the amount of deferred taxation which would otherwise be written back. Provision for deferred taxation on accelerated capital allowances has not now to be made if the tax benefit can be expected to be retained in the future through the offsetting of timing differences of the same type. It is the duty of directors to assess the probability of this in the light of their current intentions and their plans for the future.

A similar situation occurs on stock appreciation relief although the calculations are different.

There is also a potential liability for tax if an asset appreciates in value and is then sold. However, the actual liability cannot arise until a disposal takes place and a false impression is given if a taxation liability is written into the accounts merely because an asset has been revalued.

Although in the several circumstances outlined above it is not necessary to provide amounts in the deferred taxation account for what appear to be liabilities which will not crystallize, the potential amount of the full deferred taxation liabilities has to be disclosed by way of a note to the accounts.

Normally, the bulk of potential liability is made up of timing differences on capital allowances and stock relief. In order to avoid payment of the deferred element, companies therefore have to keep up their annual purchases of machinery and stock. Directors calculate the amount of deferred tax payable in the foreseeable future on the basis of the company being a going concern and continuing at the existing level of activity.

A banker must therefore look closely at the amount of the deferred tax as it appears in the balance sheet and compare it with the full liability as stated in the notes to the accounts. If the company's affairs are well run and the going concern basis is not in question, the liability as stated in the balance sheet can be accepted. If, however, there are doubts about management ability and the company is running down, a banker must be aware that further sums could become due in tax. Capital allowances on plant and machinery are being phased out (Finance Act 1986) but bankers must be aware of their effect in case a similar arrangement is reintroduced at some future time.

Conduct of the account
The banker has one very great advantage over other students of balance sheets or providers of finance for businesses in that he is in daily touch with the borrower's banking account, which discloses both the turnover and the average overdraft. Any really pronounced increase in the average debit balance on an overdrawn account should always be investigated and suitable enquiries made if the reason is not obvious. If an increased average overdraft is accompanied by the development of a 'hard core' in a borrowing which formerly fluctuated, and is associated with a sharp increase in turnover, overtrading may be the cause. The same phenomena

but without increase of turnover may indicate purchase of fixed assets, failure of stocks to move off, or investments in or loans to other companies. A falling turnover with a rising average overdraft often indicates that losses are being incurred and may throw doubt upon the saleability of stocks.

LANCASHIRE POLYTECHNIC LLRS

III

Purpose of the bank advance

Security, it has been well said, means freedom from worry. A balance sheet is not a security and when a banker lends money because he has heard an acceptable proposition and has seen a balance sheet which he thinks adequately strong to support it, he cannot dismiss certain worries from his mind with the nonchalance that he could display if he had obtained a charge over something solid and tangible. He is much more in the hands of his customer and if he allows himself to be led away by some smooth fairy tale he may have cause for regret.

To take a simple instance: suppose a customer borrows £7,000, saying that he wants it for use in his business, and gives the bank security in the form of a mortgage over a house worth £30,000. The banker might justifiably feel annoyed if he found that the customer had not used the money in the business at all, but had gambled it away at the dogs or had spent it on gifts of jewellery for some frivolous acquaintance. But he need not worry about the safety of the advance; at a pinch he could obtain repayment by selling the house. If, however, the £7,000 had been lent without security, and upon the strength of a balance sheet, the banker's emotions might amount to something more dire than mere annoyance. The money which he thought would be profitably employed in the business has been frittered away and instead of helping to strengthen the balance sheet the banking facilities have helped to weaken it.

A balance sheet cannot be expected to disclose whether or not a customer is truthful; the banker must make up his own mind on that score and if in doubt he should not lend—or at least not without adequate tangible security. A more difficult situation arises where an unsecured lending is genuinely required for business purposes and would be justifiable if the money were employed in certain ways, but not if it were used differently. For instance, an overdraft limit which could be quite happily granted to finance a thriving company's increasing turnover might be declined if it were needed by the same company to enable it to repay directors' loans or to distribute a large dividend. Generally speaking, a bank will be more ready to lend money which is to stay in the borrower's business (i.e., which is to be matched by an increase in current or fixed assets) than to lend so that other liabilities may be reduced. Customers very often do not appreciate this distinction. They tend to think that banks assess the creditworthiness of a business as an amount of money, without regard to the purpose to which it is to be applied; and if, without adequate enquiry, a banker jumps to the conclusion that his money is intended to increase business activity, and finds out too late that it has been used to pay off pressing creditors, or to enable the company to buy a new Mercedes for the managing director, he has only himself to blame.

Beware, therefore, of vague generalities and of the traditional clichés which so often appear upon applications sent by a branch for the sanction of head office: 'The advance is required for business purposes' or some similar formula, unelaborated and unadorned. Payment of corporation tax or VAT is a legitimate 'business purpose' but it is important for a banker to distinguish between finance to enable tax to be paid when it falls due and finance for payment of tax which is in arrear. The former is very often financed temporarily by means of a bank overdraft, which is usually repaid within quite a short time by the inflow of (not yet taxable) earnings. Payment of arrears of tax is a very different matter; if it has not been possible to pay off the tax in the ordinary course of business, how will it be possible to pay off the overdraft? A banker who steps unwittingly into the taxgatherer's shoes may find that it is not easy to step out again.

Working capital or fixed capital
The banker, obviously, should always ascertain whether his money is to be used to swell the assets of the borrower or to decrease outstanding liabilities. If it is to swell the assets he should also ascertain whether it is to finance current assets or fixed assets. Once again 'business purposes', which would cover either case, is a formula too vague to be useful. Purchase of plant; extension of a factory; launching a large advertising campaign; acquiring the goodwill of a rival business; these are all perfectly normal business purposes and no customer need feel embarrassed at asking for bank finance to help with them. But a banker will realize that a purchase of fixed or intangible assets with bank money will reduce the liquidity of the borrower's balance sheet and in some cases will create an unliquid position. This is an important consideration when deciding whether or not to lend and should never be overlooked. Sometimes it is necessary to stipulate, when granting a limit, that the bank's money shall not be used to finance the acquisition of fixed assets or other businesses.

But, it may be objected, suppose a banker grants an overdraft limit for one purpose and it is used for another. Will he remain in ignorance of what has happened until he sees the next balance sheet? And will it not then be too late to take any effective action? These are cogent questions. Let us take the first one first.

The banker will guess that something has gone awry when he finds that the banking account is not running in accordance with his expectations. Substantial expenditure on fixed assets or intangibles, if financed from bank money, will give rise to a 'hard core' in the overdraft (i.e., a point below which the overdraft does not dip) and a heavier average borrowing.

Drawing on bank facilities to pay off loan creditors or arrears of tax would have a similar effect, and so, also, would losses in trading. Faced with a marked change in the working of an account, the banker should endeavour to track down the cause by examining the transactions which pass through his hands and ascertaining the names of payees of large cheques. If these do not supply answers to the questions in his mind, he can always ask his customer what is going on. Failure to notice a really marked and substantial change in the working of an account, or, having noticed it, failure to establish the true cause, is a very common background to bad debts and troublesome accounts.

The fact that accounts are now produced by computers instead of by ledger clerks means that the customers' accounts are not now so easily seen by bank staff and by managers. This, however, can be overcome by a routine examination of the paper vouchers which are used to pass entries to customers' accounts (i.e., cheques and credit slips etc.) and an examination of statement sheets before they are passed to customers. As progress is made more entries will in future be made without the use of paper vouchers but managers must not let the examination of accounts be overlooked unless they wish to discard the very useful forewarning of trouble which this can give.

In a pronounced case of misuse of a bank advance, the banker ought certainly to be able to find out what is happening without waiting for the balance sheet. He has a fund of local knowledge to draw upon as well as the picture shown by the banking account. Can he take any effective action? Where there has been a clear breach of a condition laid down by the banker when he agreed to lend the money, there is always the remedy of calling in the advance. Few bankers, however, would act drastically or hastily in such a situation. Disapproval would probably be voiced, and there would be pressure for reductions. If disregard of the bank's wishes had been particularly blatant some additional control over the future drawing of cheques might be insisted upon. Fortunately, there are few customers who would deliberately flout the expressed terms of an advance made by a bank; and the few that might not scruple to do so are perhaps deterred by the thought that a banker's confidence, once destroyed, is difficult to rebuild.

CASE 5

We will now look at two different propositions for the same company. The amount required for each proposition is the same but the purpose is different and it is the purpose which is important as this has a bearing not only on the safety of the advance but on the way in which a company will develop.

A banker does not lend against a balance sheet but against a proposition, as this case will illustrate.

Frost and Snow Limited are manufacturers of imitation leather goods. They have been in business for 10 years and although three hardworking directors comprise the executive team, there are two other part-time non-executive directors who have provided most of the share capital. A summary of the company's balance sheet is as follows:

FROST AND SNOW LTD.

	£		£
Cash	4,013	Trade creditors	25,012
Debtors	33,232	Bank	21,103
Work in progress	20,105	Corporation tax	4,237
Stock	28,020	Dividend	5,000
	85,370		55,352
		Mortgage loan	40,018
			95,370
Freehold factory	70,000	Capital	50,000
Plant and machinery		Reserves	36,800
fixtures and fittings	20,370	Profit and loss account	3,200
Vehicles	9,630		
	£185,370		£185,370

Sales	£400,000	Profit for year	£6,520
		after	
		tax	£4,237
		depreciation	£3,170
		directors' remuneration	£35,000

At present the company enjoys an unsecured bank overdraft limit of £30,000 for normal trading. As a start it would be as well to examine this aspect. The total amount of current liabilities is therefore approximately £55,000, against which there are £85,000 of current assets. A good liquid position is therefore evident and substantial proprietor's funds of approximately £90,000 provide a good cushion against adversity. Sales are £400,000 per annum (an average of £33,000 per month) which should ensure plenty of movement and swing in the account. Debtors and stock seem reasonable on this monthly turnover. Debtors are in excess of creditors and a profit is being made. In all, a reasonable position is evident from the bank's point of view.

Now to consider the two propositions.

Proposition 1

The directors say that trade is good and orders in hand will ensure that turnover will rise by 15 per cent. in the coming year. Additionally, they wish to start selling their products in a new geographical area in the United Kingdom in which they have not sold before. This will also increase sales by possibly a further 15 per cent. Some re-arrangement of factory space will be necessary which will involve building costs of £10,000 and a further £30,000 will be required to support additional debtors, stock and work in progress. A good increase in profits is anticipated and the directors have agreed not to increase the dividend for at least two years. In all, a new limit of £70,000 is requested and the bank is offered a debenture as security.

Proposition 2

This request is also for a new limit of £70,000 with a debenture as security. The request on this proposition is because the factory is too small, a staff canteen is to be provided, and vehicles need replacing. The cost of the extensions is estimated at £30,000 (but the mortgage loan can be increased by £10,000 to £50,000), the staff canteen will cost £10,000 and the replacement vehicles will also cost £10,000.

Proposition 1 causes the bank no difficulty. The business is healthy and the higher limit is to support further profitable activity and thereby enable funds to be generated which will be retained by the company. The movement and swing in the account should increase as also should the excess of current assets over current liabilities. With a debenture, the bank will have adequate security.

Proposition 2: In this case all the additional expenditure will be on fixed assets. It may well be desirable to extend the factory, provide a staff canteen and replace the vehicles but this expenditure of itself will not increase trade. It will involve the company in additional expense for interest due to the bank. With so little plough back of profits after payment of dividend, there will be insufficient funds to meet this extra expense. Hardcore lending will then occur. If this proposition were agreed by the bank, the summary of the balance sheet could be adjusted to show the resultant position as follows:

FROST AND SNOW LTD.

	£		£
Cash	4,013	Trade creditors	25,012
Debtors	33,232	Bank	61,103
Work in progress	20,105	Corporation tax	4,237
Stock	28,020	Dividend	5,000
	85,370		95,352
		Mortgage loan	50,018
			145,370
Freehold factory	107,000	Capital	50,000
Plant, machinery,		Reserves	36,800
fixtures & fittings	23,370	Profit and loss account	3,200
Vehicles	19,630		
			£235,370
	£235,370		

For this illustration it has been assumed that £3,000 of the expenditure on the canteen came into the category of fixtures and fittings and the remainder increased the amount of the freehold factory. The debenture will provide the bank with adequate security but the figure for net current assets indicates the difficulties which will occur. The current liabilities total £95,000 whereas the current assets are insufficient to cover this amount. With an overdraft limit of £70,000 the company will be able to pay the dividend and tax due. As debtors exceed creditors there should be no difficulty in that direction either. The only trouble will be with the bank overdraft which will contain a large element of solid borrowing with no hope of reduction. The retained profit after dividend of £1,520 will be insufficient to meet the cost of the additional borrowing.

It should not be assumed from a study of this case that overdraft lending for the purchase of fixed assets is wrong. All the surrounding aspects have to be considered. If a company is able to generate sufficient funds to repay in a few years any solid borrowing that might result, an overdraft facility is quite satisfactory.

In the present case the generation of sufficient funds is lacking. Rectification might be possible by lending yet a further sum to develop the trade of the business but this, of course, would need further consideration of the prospects.

Consequences of illiquidity

Where a balance sheet discloses an unliquid position the stability of a business must always be suspect. Creditors may want their money without delay—they themselves may have come under pressure from their own creditors—and if the total of current assets is less than the total of current liabilities a dangerous situation can quickly arise. It should be borne in mind, however, that deferred or medium-term liabilities are not current liabilities in the strict sense. For example, the holder of a debenture repayable in twenty annual instalments cannot normally call for immediate repayment in full unless the instalments or the interest payments fall into arrear or the business is on the point of breaking down. A liability secured by a mortgage may similarly be of a long- or medium-term nature; the balance sheets of property-owning companies, for instance, commonly disclose an unliquid position which is, nevertheless, quite stable and satisfactory if the mortgages can be serviced out of rents receivable. Where those liabilities which are strictly due for current payment exceed the total of current assets, there is definite instability and the business is vulnerable to pressure from its creditors.

The converse, however, is not necessarily true, and a clear and substantial excess of current assets over current liabilities is no guarantee of stability or of invulnerability. A great deal depends upon how current the current assets really are; in other words, how frequently they are turning over and turning into cash. The following example shows a balance sheet with a total of current assets twice the total of current liabilities, nevertheless the company has got itself into an extremely vulnerable position.

CASE 6

Quetzal Quail & Co. Ltd. is a private company manufacturing cut leather soles. The business was started ten years ago by two friends who had learned the trade in their employment with other firms. Capital was available, good profits were earned and a fair proportion left in the business. An unsecured overdraft limit of £14,000 was granted some years ago and has been renewed from time to time. Formerly the account fluctuated well and credit balances were seen, but the advance has now developed a 'hard core' of about £16,000 and there have been excesses.

The bank is asked to increase the limit to £50,000 to enable the company to buy leather to fill firm orders.

QUETZAL QUAIL AND CO. LTD.

Manufacturers of cut leather soles

	£		£
Cash	234	Trade creditors	41,558
Debtors	36,824	Bank	20,160
Stock	104,494	Corporation tax—3 months	8,316
	141,552		70,034
		Corporation tax—15 months	8,280
			78,314
Machinery etc.	12,576	Capital	48,000
Vehicles	10,482	Reserves	19,400
Prepayments	720	Profit and loss account	19,616
	£165,330		£165,330
Sales	£348,000	Profit for year	£12,510
		after	
		tax	£8,280
		depreciation	2,196
		directors' remuneration	£30,994

The surplus shown in the balance sheet is about £87,000 and the net current assets £71,000. The relationship of debtors to sales is satisfactory but, on the balance sheet date, trade creditors exceed debtors by £4,700, a fact which calls for some explanation.

The outstanding item is, of course, the figure for stock, which dominates the whole picture and is £17,000 in excess of the surplus. And the increase in the overdraft is required for the purchase of yet more stock! Something is obviously out of gear and the most probable explanation is that the wrong raw materials have been purchased in the past and have failed to move off. Enquiry of the directors and a comparison with the balance sheets of earlier years will be necessary. On the face of things there may be £70,000 of stock which is not turning over at all.

Situations like this are not uncommon and the directors usually say that the surplus stocks are held as a reserve and are worth far more than the figure shown in the balance sheet. That may well be, but even so it is not a banker's function to finance the holding of stocks which are not turning over and are unnecessarily high for the business. If customers wish to invest in (or to speculate in) commodities they should not expect their bankers to put up the finance. It is far too risky a pursuit for a prudent banker. Prices can fall as well as rise, and inflation does not bring with it a perpetual and unbroken bull-market for stockpilers. Leather, wool, cotton and many other staple commodities often show spectacular fluctuations in price over a period of time.

Causes of vulnerability

A business may be vulnerable, then, if it is not turning over its stock-in-trade quickly enough, even though the balance sheet shows a liquid surplus. The logical way to look at liquidity, in such cases, is to consider the surplus stock as a non-quoted investment and (mentally) not to include it in the current assets.

Vulnerability may also arise in the following cases:

(i) Where too long a period of credit is allowed. This will attract weak purchasers and will be evidenced by too high a figure for debtors in the balance sheet. Sometimes a favoured debtor receives special terms and such arrangements can be dangerous, particularly where the favoured debtor is another company and the two companies have an interlocking or related directorate.

(ii) Where there is one predominant creditor or one predominant debtor. This cannot be seen from the balance sheet; the banker should either know the facts from the banking account or make suitable enquiries of the directors. A predominant creditor may suddenly call for his money or refuse further credit; a predominant debtor may fail or demand longer credit. Either may enforce harsh terms and cut profits down to the bone.

(iii) Where good profits have been made and have been sunk in fixed assets without regard to the eventual tax liability. This is particularly dangerous if profits subsequently fall away.

(iv) Where a trade is subject to fluctuations of taste or fashion.

(v) Where a comparatively small business is trying to make headway amongst much larger competitors.

(vi) Where a business depends wholly upon the skill or flair of one man.

Strictly speaking, not all these points are directly connected with balance sheets, but nevertheless they are very relevant to the interpretation of balance sheets in relation to the assessment of banking propositions and banking risks. The list is not and could not be exhaustive, nor is it suggested that a business which is vulnerable is necessarily not creditworthy. Banks, like other businesses, expect to undertake a certain amount of risk; the important thing is that when they do so they should be able to see their risks as clearly as possible and weigh them up with care and understanding.

Banking—the lending of money by banks—is not an exact science; despite all study and analysis there always remains room for differences of opinion and what appeals to one banker as good business may strike another as an unjustifiable adventure. Nowadays banks compete strongly for borrowing accounts, and, provided that a banking proposition does not conflict with whatever directives the Chancellor of the Exchequer may issue from time to time, it must be unattractive indeed if no clearing bank is willing to agree to it.

IV

Past records

In making commercial lendings, especially without security, a banker traditionally pays particular regard to the 'three Cs' of the borrower—Character, Capital and Competence. Borrowers, on the other hand, are said to seek bankers who display faith, hope and charity.

A borrower's balance sheet, although only one of several sources of information, is of considerable help in the assessment of all three of the 'Cs'; and a series of balance sheets, extending over three years or more, is still more informative. Capital in this context means, of course, the surplus shown in the balance sheet. A sequence of balance sheets discloses not only the amount of the surplus at the balance sheet date, but also whether it has been increasing or decreasing from year to year during the period.

Competence is denoted, or suggested, by success, especially steady and repeated success. A consistently good profits record, extending over a long period of years, constitutes powerful evidence of the competence of those in control of a business. For this purpose the record of three years is hardly enough and it is best to examine results over a period sufficiently long to ensure the inclusion of years when trading was difficult as well as times of easy prosperity.

A series of balance sheets and their accompanying accounts supply numerous pointers to character. Prudence, extravagance, rashness, ambition, optimism, selfishness, unscrupulousness and many more characteristics may be suggested by or inferred from the figures. It is desirable, however, to stress once again the danger of reading too much into balance sheets; there is no substitute for knowing one's man, and inferences based solely upon the figures can be seriously misleading.

Analysis of past trends

Trends and variations are shown up clearly by summarizing a sequence of balance sheets in parallel columns. An example is given on page 45 and for ease of reference a few comments are added there.

When an established customer wishes to borrow for the first time, or where a commercial account is offered by transfer from another bank, with a request for an advance, balance sheets for at least three years should always be seen and compared. To rely upon the latest balance sheet alone is imprudent without knowledge of what has gone before.

Broadly speaking, the trends which require examination when a sequence of balance sheets is under scrutiny fall into the same groups as the figures of a single balance sheet and it is convenient to examine them in a regular order:

> (i) surplus;
>
> (ii) liquidity;
>
> (iii) prior charges (mortgages, etc.);
>
> (iv) trading figures;
>
> (v) profits record;
>
> (vi) any special items.

(i) *The Surplus.* No variation in the amount of the surplus can take place without cause. There are, in fact, surprisingly few ways by which a change in the surplus can be brought about, as a few moments' reflection will verify, and the source and circumstances of any change should always be ascertained and considered. The most common cause is profits or losses arising in the ordinary running of the business, and to a prospective lender there are few signs more encouraging than a steady rise in the surplus over a period of years, resulting from the retention of profits.

The issue of additional capital is another source of increase in the surplus, although trading losses, if any have been incurred, will naturally go to offset such increase. An issue of capital should be specially noted on the balance sheet summary and the note should state whether the issue brought new cash into the business, whether it represented capitalization of loan money already employed, or whether it arose upon the transfer of physical assets from, or upon amalgamation with, another company.

Sometimes the surplus is increased as the result of a revaluation of fixed assets. This is not a positive sign if the object is merely to make the balance sheet figures look larger and more imposing, but when it occurs in the course of an amalgamation or reorganization it is very often a necessity of accounting. The full story should be ascertained and briefly noted.

Refunds of taxation, or the release of provisions set up in the past for taxation or for other contingencies, may also increase the surplus, and conversely any new provisions will normally decrease it unless they are taken from the undistributed profits of the year covered by the accounts.

(ii) *Liquidity.* If the summary discloses a marked change in the amount of the liquid surplus the cause should be ascertained and noted. Capital expenditure is the most usual cause of a reduction; others are trading losses or bad debts, trade investments, and the distribution of profits accumulated in previous years. An increase in the liquid surplus may be due to the earning and retention of profits, the sale of capital assets or trade investments, the repayment of loans, or the introduction of additional capital.

Besides changes in the amount of the liquid surplus, changes in its relation to the total of current liabilities should also be considered. Obviously a liquid surplus of £5,000 which would be comfortable when current liabilities were £10,000 would become very thin if current liabilities rose to, say, £60,000. The proportion which the liquid surplus bears to the current liabilities should therefore be carefully watched and the effect of any marked change should be assessed. Deterioration in the *proportion* (as distinct from the amount) of the liquid surplus is one of the results of an increase in turnover without an increase in capital resources and it may, therefore, be one of the early signs of overtrading. However, each case must be judged on its facts and merits. A declining turnover may improve the liquidity ratio, but may nevertheless indicate a state of affairs more unhealthy than a modest amount of overtrading.

(iii) *Prior charges.* Any mortgages or charges should be considered and details noted if the amount is large. Generally speaking, banks do not expect to lend without security if other creditors are secured. It should be remembered that assets may have become encumbered since the date of the last balance sheet, and whilst there is not much risk of this having been done without the banker's knowledge where he is lending to a customer whose account he already has, enquiry or search may be desirable where he is taking over an account from another bank.

(iv) *Trading figures* (creditors, debtors, stock, work in progress). Any marked changes should be scrutinized, particularly where one or more of the categories starts 'ballooning'. Watch should also be kept upon the trend of the following relationships:

    (*a*) trade creditors to debtors;

    (*b*) debtors to sales

    (*c*) stock to sales.

If bills payable or bills receivable start appearing where there have been none previously, or if the company starts selling its book debts, the circumstances should be ascertained and recorded.

43

(v) *Profits record.* The size, trend, and steadiness of results should be observed and also the extent to which profits are retained, especially in a business which is owned by its directors.

Profits figures are often affected by special items—refunds of tax profits on sale of vehicles or surplus machinery, compensation to outgoing directors, expensive lawsuits, etc. It is advisable to deal with items of this kind by means of a special note, otherwise the true trading results of different years will not be readily comparable.

(vi) *Special items.* Every large item in any balance sheet should be examined and considered, and similarly any substantial change in such an item should be weighed up when a sequence of balance sheets is under review. 'Ballooning' should be watched for, especially in the stock figure or in amounts owing by or invested in associated companies. No value should be attached to the latter items unless the balance sheets of the associated companies are produced or some other reliable information about them is available.

NOTES
ON FIREBIRD AND ROC LTD BALANCE SHEETS

These balance sheets show a picture of a progressive company with well-managed finances. Turnover has expanded rapidly, but retained profits have been sufficient to keep the trading figures in a healthy state, and the liquid surplus has increased in amount; moreover its proportion to current liabilities also shows an increase. A second factory, and the additional machinery to cope with the increasing output, were purchased in Year B from the proceeds of an issue of preference capital for cash, the result in the balance sheet being an increase in the surplus and an increase in fixed assets.

The capital shows an increase of £90,000 in Year C, arising by way of a two-for-one bonus issue of ordinary shares. This amounts to a transference of £90,000 from reserves to capital and does not increase the surplus nor alter the assets side of the balance sheet.

The capital reserve of £240,000 arises out of a revaluation of fixed assets. It increases the surplus (on paper), but has no effect on the physical assets of the business, nor its earning capacity.

Firebird & Roc Ltd. is a private company and the bonus issue and revaluation may suggest that the directors intend to apply for the shares to be quoted on one of the recognized stock exchanges.

CASE 7

FIREBIRD AND ROC LTD.

	Year A £	Year B £	Year C £
Cash	701	375	480
Debtors	46,983	57,290	67,737
Stock and Work in progress	58,011	81,398	114,819
	105,695	139,063	183,036
Land and Buildings	60,980	135,400(d)	300,000
Machinery and Plant	40,334	69,533	138,682(e)
	£207,009	£343,996	£621,718
Turnover (sales)	£410,000	£540,000	£680,000

	Year A £	Year B £	Year C £
Creditors within one year	35,987	46,012	50,839
Bank	18,998	31,780	31,654
Tax—Current	2,000	2,300	2,900
Proposed Dividends	2,723	2,723	2,723
	59,708	82,815	88,116
Creditors due after one year	5,000	4,500	4,000
Deferred Tax	4,500	7,700	20,100
Capital	69,208	95,015	112,216
Capital Reserve	45,000	145,000(a)	235,000(b)
			240,000(c)
Revenue Reserves	90,000	100,000	30,000
Profit and loss account	2,801	3,981	4,502
	£207,009	£343,996	£621,718
Profit	£7,210	£17,203	£26,544
after tax of	£6,400	£9,800	£23,474

Notes (a) £100,000 preference capital issued for cash.
(b) £90,000 capitalised from reserves.
(c) Surplus arising on revaluation of buildings and plant.
(d) Another factory purchased.

(e) Buildings £137,399 written up to £300,000
    Plant   £61,283 ditto   £138,682
                 £198,682   £438,682

Net increase, see note (c) £240,000

45

Group accounts

The linking up of businesses through association of companies produces many financial complexities. The association most commonly found, although it is by no means the only one, comprises a holding company and one or more subsidiary companies. Some of these organizations are gigantic financial empires, others are of rather less importance, others again are quite small. Perhaps the small and medium-sized organizations give the banker more difficulty. He may be asked to lend to a subsidiary company and upon examining its balance sheet may find that the principal asset is money owing by a second subsidiary in the same group; the balance sheet of the second subsidiary could show substantial sums owing by a third and a fourth member of the group; their balance sheets may show large loans to the holding company; the balance sheet of the holding company may disclose no assets except shares in and loans to its various subsidiaries.

There is no need for suspicion nor for despair. If the affairs of a company are inextricably interwoven with those of other members of the same group the banker's best plan is to turn his attention to the financial position of the group as a whole and to endeavour to frame answers to the following questions:

(i) What are the true assets and liabilities of *the group,* i.e., after excluding debts and investments within the group itself?

(ii) Is the proposed limit justifiable in relation to the financial position of the group, and what other bank accommodation is there available to the group?

(iii) Is the plan for repayment practicable out of group finances?

(iv) Can the banker rely upon those who are in control of the group to carry out the plan for repayment?

(v) Is security necessary and, if so, is it available?

To obtain an overall view of the assets and liabilities of the group, the banker should examine the consolidated balance sheet. In this the inter-company indebtedness will have been omitted (it cancels out) and broadly speaking the consolidated figures will show the financial position of the group in relation to the outside world, much as though all the companies were one. A consolidated balance sheet is not the actual balance sheet of any company nor of any legal entity; it is simply a summarized statement of the group position. Thus, the banker is able to obtain answers to his first three questions (except the second part of question (ii)) from the consolidated balance sheet. Accommodation available at other banks should be the subject of enquiry of the directors.

However, that is not the end of the task. If the proposed borrowing looks acceptable in relation to the group's figures, the banker has still to decide what position he wishes to occupy in the group's financial structure. He cannot lend to a consolidated balance sheet. He lends, if at all, to one or more of the companies in the group. What possibilities are open to him and what do they involve?

   (i) He could lend without security to one of the companies. To do so without misgiving he would have to feel completely satisfied that the group could easily repay him and that those in charge would undoubtedly see to it that money came to him for that purpose.

   (ii) He could lend as in (i) but with the added support of a guarantee by the directors.

  (iii) He could lend to a subsidiary with the support of a guarantee by the parent company. This would, in effect, put the consolidated surplus behind him; he would have that to fall back upon. Of course, he would have no direct claim against the assets of the other companies in the group, but in the event of disaster he could not lose any money until the whole of the consolidated surplus had been lost. Note, however, that minority interests in subsidiary companies do not form part of the consolidated surplus, and will not be behind the guarantee.

Much the same situation would result if the banker lent to the parent company without security.

  (iv) He could lend to one company with the support of a guarantee by each of the other members of the group. He would then be able to call upon any or all of the companies for repayment of the advance, and in liquidation proceedings he could prove for his debt alongside the creditors of each company. Thus wherever in the group there were realizable assets to be found he would be able to put in a claim to a share of their value.

     Very often where a group of companies borrow from one bank cross-guarantees are taken, each company guaranteeing each other company. If this is done, the banker's technical position in a liquidation would be quite a good one. For the full total owing to him by the group he would be entitled to receive a dividend in the £ at a rate no worse than the best dividend paid by any of the companies to its other unsecured creditors. He might receive more, but could not be compelled to accept less.

     With cross-guarantees it is convenient for the banker to asses his risk by regarding himself as an unsecured creditor on the consolidated balance sheet for his aggregate lending to the group. It is long odds that his technical position would be better than that in case of disaster, and such an assessment is, therefore, on the cautious side. Minority interests, in such a case, would not be in conflict with the bank and could be regarded as forming an addition to the consolidated surplus.

(v) He could stipulate for tangible security.

(vi) The strongest position of all is where the banker obtains cross-guarantees, as in (iv), and these are supported by debentures on all the companies. With cross-guarantees and debentures he is broadly in the position of a debenture-creditor on the consolidated balance sheet for his aggregate lending to the group.

Various permutations and combinations of the foregoing points may arise in practice: for example, guarantees by some fellow subsidiaries but not all; a debenture by the parent company but not by the subsidiaries; guarantees covering only part of the limit granted, etc. Quite frequently these midway positions represent a compromise between what the banker would have liked to obtain by way of security and what the directors were prepared to offer.

Where a debenture by the parent company is held it should be remembered that this is more than merely a power to realize that company's assets. A standard form of debenture used by a bank would normally include powers adequate in case of need to enable the bank to control and manage the parent company and, through it, the business of the whole group.

CASE 8

After all this theorizing it may, perhaps, be a relief to turn to another illustration.

Kittiwake Kite & Buzzard Ltd. is a private company of manufacturing clothiers. The account was obtained from another bank, and although the limit has been twice increased during its twelve-months run and now stands at £120,000, it has not proved sufficient and there have been frequent excesses. The directors are energetic young men, able, ambitious and secretive. It is known that certain retailing subsidiary companies have been acquired in the past, but the accounts are with other banks. The £120,000 limit is secured by a debenture and the branch manager has been eagerly awaiting the new balance sheet, as the directors have told him that they have had a most successful year. When it arrives his heart sinks.

KITTIWAKE KITE AND BUZZARD LTD.

Manufacturing clothiers

	£		£
Cash	48	Trade creditors	50,028
Debtors	63,708	Bank	123,076
Stock	113,148	Tax—current	33,824
	176,904		206,928
		Deferred tax	4,716
			211,644
Land and buildings	39,364	Capital	47,000
Machinery & plant etc.	29,000	Capital reserves	4,212
Due from subsidiaries	12,196	Profit and loss account	66,708
Shares in subsidiaries	72,100		£329,564
	£329,564		
Sales	£786,000	Loss for year	£3,556
		after	
		tax	£4,716
		depreciation	£7,172
		directors' remuneration	£35,000
		and after writing off stock	£18,116

The directors explain that the writing down of stock is purely a precautionary measure and say that in reality the current value is about £180,000. The true trading results for the year, they say, were excellent. The branch manager is still not happy. The balance sheet shows an immediate tax liability of £33,824 with no obvious liquid resources to meet it; the directors agree that they are being pressed and ask to have the limit increased to £160,000, adding airily that the shares in subsidiary companies are worth 'many times the balance sheet figure'.

Under pressure, they eventually produce the consolidated balance sheet of the group (see page 50).

The consolidated surplus is £200,000 after deduction of intangibles. There are net current assets of £162,000, but the stock figure is very high. The trade investments prove upon enquiry to be quoted and marketable with no adverse effect on the company if they were sold. The amount could therefore be added to the net current assets. The current liabilities, excluding the secured loans, are £380,000 and the current assets, including the investments, £570,000, giving a substantial liquid surplus, though the heavy stock figure must not be overlooked, nor the taxation liability. Trade creditors of the group exceed group debtors, but the debtors of the retailing companies are naturally not large.

49

KITTIWAKE KITE AND BUZZARD LTD.
AND ITS SUBSIDIARY COMPANIES

CONSOLIDATED BALANCE SHEET

	£		£
Cash	44,356	Trade creditors	136,184
Debtors	84,588	Banks	151,304
Stock	413,200	Tax—current	91,288
		Dividends	1,420
	542,144		380,196
		Secured loans	79,000
		Deferred tax	19,312
		Minority interests in subsidiaries	83,908
			562,416
Land & buildings	135,812	Capital	47,000
Machinery, plant, fittings, etc.	56,504	Capital reserve	105,192
Trade investments	28,240	Profit and loss account	90,856
Premiums on acquisitions of shares in subsidiaries	32,768		
Goodwill	9,996		
	£805,464		£805,464

Consolidated profit figures not produced

The capital reserve of £105,000 has arisen from the sale by one of the retailing companies of certain freehold shop properties, on a return-lease basis, for more than balance sheet value. The directors say that further sales by another subsidiary are pending and that these will bring £160,000 liquid cash into the group after clearing the secured loans. They promise a reduction of £50,000 in the limit of the parent company.

It must be borne in mind that as the goodwill and the premiums on acquisition of shares have not been written off to reserves they must be written down annually over their economic life by debits to the profit and loss account. This will affect the future profits but no cash will leave the group in consequence.

It should also be borne in mind that the debenture does not cover all the assets shown in the consolidated figures, but, nevertheless, the branch manager would feel a good deal happier on seeing the complete picture, which discloses a more substantial position than might be expected from an examination of the parent company's balance sheet only.

In many instances the opposite occurs, and the consolidated figures disclose more strain on the finances than the parent company's balance sheet would lead one to expect.

The essential thing in dealing with group finances is to ascertain and weigh up the true assets and liabilities of the group, and then to attempt to envisage the whole in some sort of perspective. Only then is it possible to judge the financial strength behind the particular company or companies for which bank accommodation is required.

Thus, for groups, as for isolated companies, there is no short cut, no formula, and no golden rule, except, perhaps: Keep on pegging away until you get a clear picture.

V

Statements of Source and Application of Funds

Although it is not a requirement of the Companies Act 1985, company accounts now have an additional set of figures attached to the usual profit and loss accounts and balance sheets. This is called a Statement of Source and Application of Funds and is a requirement specified by the Statement of Standard Accounting Practice No. 10 (SSAP 10).

This is an important statement from a banker's point of view as it enables him to comprehend in greater depth what has been taking place in the financial period covered by the accounts.

We will now examine the accounts for two years of a public limited company. These are set out in one of the formats specified by the Companies Act 1985 and, at first sight, appear to be more complicated than the simple balance sheets we have so far examined. However, once the analysis is carried out according to our normal method it will be seen that the apparent complications disappear. In most company accounts only overall figures are given for each heading but further details are provided in notes to the accounts. Although notes to the accounts are not produced in this example it is always necessary to read the notes thoroughly for a full understanding to be obtained.

CASE 9   LEADER AND COMPANY PLC
Manufacturers of electrical equipment

	Year A (£'000)		Year B (£'000)	
Fixed assets				
Tangible assets				
Freehold land and buildings		240		240
Plant and machinery		120		112
Fixtures, fittings, tools & equipment		160		168
Total tangible assets		520		520
Current assets				
Stocks				
Raw materials and consumables	580		630	
Work in progress	500		550	
Finished goods and goods for resale	600		660	
		1,680		1,840
Debtors				
Trade debtors	900		980	
Prepayments and accrued income	60		100	
		960		1,080
Total current assets		2,640		2,920
Creditors—amounts falling due within twelve months				
Bank loans and overdrafts	440		640	
Trade creditors	1,500		1,700	
Other creditors—loan stock	80		120	
		2,020		2,460
Net current assets		620		460
Total assets less current liabilities		1,140		980
Creditors falling due after more than one year				
Loan stock	120			
Other creditors including taxation and social security	100		100	
		220		100
		£920		£880
Capital and reserves				
Called up share capital		200		200
Reserves—general		500		500
Profit and loss account		220		180
		£920		£880
Sales		£8.2m		£7.5m
Profit (loss)		£20,000		(£40,000)
after				
depreciation		£64,000		£64,000
directors' remuneration		£132,000		£120,000
tax		nil		nil

The analysis of year B of this balance sheet under our short analysis method will be as follows:

	(£'000)		(£'000)
Debtors	1,080	Bank	640
Stocks	1,840	Trade creditors	1,700
		Other creditors	120
	2,920		2,460
		Longer term creditors	100
			2,560
Freeholds	240	Capital	200
Plant and machinery	112	Reserves	500
Fixtures, fittings, tools and		Profit and loss account	180
equipment	168		
	£3,440		£3,440

Sales	£7.5m
Loss for year	£40,000
after	
depreciation	£64,000
directors' remuneration	£120,000
taxation	nil

In this form it is much easier to see the salient points;
1. Net current assets are £460,000.
2. Trade creditors are much in excess of debtors.
3. A loss, albeit, a small one has been made.
4. The bank overdraft at £640,000 is far greater than the whole of the fixed assets and not far short of the amount of the proprietors' funds.

Obviously some explanation is required from the directors but before doing this it would be as well to look at the Statement of Source and Application of Funds. First, let us consider how it is compiled.

The differences for figures for assets and liabilities are compared for two consecutive financial periods after taking into account the profit or loss made in the financial period under review. Also we want to know of any movements in the profit and loss account which are book entries and do not therefore involve the movement of funds; we also wish to know how such entries have been applied. In this case we see that there is an entry for depreciation for £64,000 and the notes to the accounts will enlighten us on how this was applied. Let us suppose that the notes show that plant and machinery were depreciated by £30,000 and fixtures, fittings, tools and equipment were depreciated by £34,000.

We now have the following information;

Loss for the year: £40,000

Depreciation written off: £64,000 (being £30,000 from plant and machinery and £34,000 from fixtures, fittings, tools and equipment)

Differences in the balance sheet of year B compared with year A;

Assets	£	
Plant and machinery	−8,000	(but depreciation was £30,000; net purchases are therefore £22,000)
Fixtures, fittings, tools and equipment	+8,000	(but depreciation was £34,000; net purchases are therefore £42,000)
Raw materials	+50,000	
Work in progress	+50,000	
Finished goods	+60,000	
Liabilities		
Bank	+200,000	
Trade creditors	+200,000	
Loan stock +40,000		
−120,000	−80,000	

From these figures a Statement of Source and Application of Funds can be produced as follows;

YEAR B

Source of funds	1
Funds generated from operations	
Loss before taxation	(40,000)
Adjustment for items not involving the movement of funds	64,000
	24,000
Taxation paid	nil
Total funds generated from operations	24,000
Increase in bank loans	200,000
Increase in trade creditors	200,000
	£424,000

Application of funds	
Purchases less disposals of plant and machinery	22,000
Purchases less disposals of fixtures, fittings, tools and equipment	42,000
Increase in raw materials	50,000
Increase in work in progress	50,000
Increase in finished goods	60,000
Increase in debtors	120,000
Decrease in loan stock	80,000
	£424,000

An examination of this statement brings out very clearly the following additional points;

1. The amount generated from operations is very small but an extra £200,000 has been drawn from the bank and creditors have been extended by an additional £200,000.

2. £64,000 has been spent on fixed assets.

3. Although the sales have decreased from £8.2m to £7.5m the stock has increased by £160,000.

4. Loan stock of £80,000 has been repaid and either the bank or the creditors have stepped into the shoes of the loan stock holders. Also the balance sheet shows that a further £120,000 of loan stock is due to be repaid in the current year.

It can now readily be appreciated that this additional set of figures is very useful to bankers.

VI

Accounting Ratios

Whenever sets of figures are produced ratios can be devised by comparing one figure with another and balance sheets and their accompanying financial statements are ideal for this practice. Each individual figure can be compared with every other figure shown and a percentage answer produced. Obviously some of the percentages produced would be meaningless but there are some ratios which can be of considerable use to understanding accounts.

Before dealing with them, however, we must keep in mind that whenever a percentage is quoted we must be alerted to considering whether that percentage is valid in the circumstances. For example, if a person borrowed 50p for a week on the understanding that he would pay back 51p at the end of the week that rate of interest would be, for practical purposes, 104% per annum, a very high rate of interest. The fact would remain that the amount involved would be only 1p. Similarly if the percentage on turnover which a business is making drops from 20% to 10% and then to 3% it does not necessarily mean that the business is heading for liquidation. It could well be that some exceptional years have occurred in the past and that the 3% may amount to £100,000 per annum for a sole proprietor and that he is quite satisfied with this figure.

Percentages must therefore be considered with caution and related to the actual figures. They do, however, throw up trends when considered year by year and can indicate lines of enquiry which can be pursued.

The most important ratios for bankers to consider are as follows;

Rate of Gross Profit. This is the percentage of gross profit to sales and is obtained by the formula,

$$\frac{\text{Gross profit} \times 100}{\text{Sales}}$$

In essence this indicates the rate of mark up which a business is able to obtain on the sale of its goods and it is a very useful ratio. It is the starting point, as from the gross profit must come all the other expenses of the business plus the remuneration for the proprietors. However, if a business sells different products its gross profit percentage will alter if there are different margins of mark up on the goods and there are changes in the proportion of goods sold. Other factors which could affect this percentage are, price cutting due to competition or a line of unsaleable stock, bad weather where seasonal considerations are important, or changes in the basis of valuation of the stock.

Often the gross profit achieved is similar in the same industry but it can also vary due to the factors mentioned above and the efficiency of the individual businesses.

A proprietor should always keep an eye on the gross profit percentage as it can alert him to possible pilferage of stock or theft of money. Similarly a banker may spot that the proprietor may be diverting sale proceeds away from the business.

Rate of Net Profit. This is the percentage of net profit to sales and is obtained by the formula,

$$\frac{\text{Net profit} \times 100}{\text{Sales}}$$

This obviously follows on from the gross profit ratio and the two ratios might be expected to work in unison. However, this is not necessarily so and a change in the net profit ratio should be examined against changes in the profit and loss account. Perhaps some expenses have got out of control or there could have been an investment in capital items, the ongoing expenses of which have not yet been matched by income.

The Current Ratio. This is obtained by the formula,

$$\frac{\text{Current assets}}{\text{Current liabilities}}$$

This is vital to the business as it deals with the complete trading aspect. For most businesses current assets will exceed current liabilities as it is from these assets that liabilities have to be met. Also as profits are generated, the current assets should increase in relation to current liabilities. However, businesses with a rapid cash intake such as supermarkets will have sold goods obtained on credit well before the creditors have to be paid and these businesses can work on a greatly different current ratio from businesses which must give credit on their sales. The current ratio cannot be accepted on its own without looking at the individual items which make up the current assets and the current liabilities. Stock does not pay wages or creditors and an increase in stock through the retention of unsaleable stock at previous valuations can improve the current ratio but be detrimental to the business. Also a director's loan in the current liabilities can sometimes be ignored if the director is not likely to or cannot withdraw it.

Rate of Stock Turnover. This can be expressed by the formula.

$$\frac{\text{Average stock of finished goods} \times 100}{\text{Cost of sales}}$$

The resultant figure shows how many days it takes to turn over the stock of finished goods and will, of course, be different for businesses looking for rapid turnover and small returns from those dealing in slower sales where the margins may be greater. It is important to use the figure for cost of sales not that for sales as the latter figure includes the profit mark up.

Although a quicker movement of stock may indicate an improvement in efficiency this will have to be related to the return obtained and also to whether adequate stock is held so that orders are not missed.

One of the disadvantages of this ratio is that it is related to average stock and this is calculated at balance sheet dates whereas the stock can vary through seasonal considerations or unexpected events such as a strike at a year end.

Debtor Ratio. This can be expressed by the formula,

$$\frac{\text{Trade debtors} \times 365}{\text{Sales}}$$

The resultant figure shows the average amount of credit given, expressed in days. Between businesses there can be considerable variation dependent upon whether cash sales form a large part of the overall business or not. Also the formula is calculated on a 'snap shot' date i.e. the date of the balance sheet which may not reflect the normal debtor position.

Creditor Ratio. This can be expressed by the formula,

$$\frac{\text{Trade creditors} \times 365}{\text{Purchases}}$$

The resultant figure shows the average length of credit taken, expressed in days. If this length increases, it could indicate that liquidity is being stretched. The amount for trade creditors must be used and not the overall figure for creditors. Some creditors may be for fixed assets and special terms may apply.

In the same way as for the debtor ratio care must be exercised as the figure for creditors is taken for one particular day.

Debtors/Creditors. This can be expressed by the formula,

$$\frac{\text{Trade debtors}}{\text{Trade creditors}}$$

If all sales are on credit and a business takes and gives credit of equal length the resultant figure will be greater than 1 as the debtors will include the gross mark up.

However, businesses vary and their terms of trade should be reflected in this ratio. A business only fails when it cannot pay its creditors and any large increase in creditors in relation to debtors must be a matter for enquiry.

59

Return on Capital Employed. This can be calculated from the formula,

$$\frac{\text{Net profit before tax} \times 100}{\text{Average of shareholders' funds}}$$

The resultant percentage will only be correct if the correct average of shareholders' funds is used. Obviously if additional funds are injected into a business during the course of the financial period an adjustment will have to be made but if the asset figures are not at correct values the figure for shareholders' funds will not be correct. However, a trend can be established and if the return on capital is good this will, of course, assist in the raising of additional funds if this should be necessary.

Gearing. This is expressed in various ways and the object of the ratio is to establish how much of the proprietors' funds are involved in a business compared to the fixed interest funds in the business. It can therefore be expressed as;

$$1. \qquad \frac{\text{Loans} \times 100}{\text{Loans and shareholders' funds}}$$

$$\text{or } 2. \qquad \frac{\text{Loans and fixed interest preference shares}}{\text{Equity funds}}$$

Although preference shares are not loans, this formula is used to show the relationship of borrowings plus fixed interest commitments to the ordinary equity funds and shows the amount of extra leverage obtained by ordinary shareholders. If profits are high the equity shareholders will obtain an increased proportion of profit compared to the other providers of funds and vice versa. This formula is, therefore, of interest to shareholders.

$$\text{or } 3. \qquad \frac{\text{Loans}}{\text{Net worth}}$$

For a banker this is the most useful way of expressing gearing. The proprietors' funds, both ordinary and fixed interest, have to be lost before loans are in danger and a banker does not normally expect to be the senior partner in an enterprise where he is not able to exercise control.

This ratio, therefore, enables him to assess the amount of risk being taken by the proprietors.

CASE 10

Let us now examine a set of accounts using our short analysis method, taking information from the Statement of Source and Application of Funds and using the ratios. Also, on this occasion we will additionally use a columnar form of analysis which was briefly mentioned earlier in this book as being more appropriate for use with complicated figures or when there are available several years of balance sheets.

HARMAN P.L.C.

	Year A £'000	Year B £'000	Year C £'000
Fixed assets			
Tangible assets			
Freeholds	1,800	3,000	4,000
Plant and machinery	4,000	4,500	6,000
Fixtures, fittings, tools and equipment	1,500	1,000	500
	7,300	8,500	10,500
Current assets			
Stocks			
Raw materials and consumables	1,200	1,700	600
Work in progress	500	600	700
Finished goods and goods for resale	1,500	1,800	3,800
Debtors			
Trade debtors	1,500	1,700	2,800
Other debtors	400	600	400
Total current assets	5,100	6,400	8,300
Creditors: amounts falling due within one year			
Bank loans and overdrafts	1,500	1,800	4,000
Trade creditors	400	500	600
Other creditors including taxation and social security	600	600	600
	2,500	2,900	5,200
Net current assets	2,600	3,500	3,100
Total assets less current liabilities	9,900	12,000	13,600
Creditors: amounts falling due after more than one year			
10% Loan stock		1,500	3,000
Other creditors including taxation and social security		100	600
	9,900	10,400	10,000
Capital and reserves			
Share capital	2,000	2,000	2,000
Reserves	7,000	7,000	7,000
Profit and loss account	900	1,400	1,000
(previous year £9,400)	9,900	10,400	10,000
Turnover (sales)	12,000	14,000	15,000
Gross profit	4,000	4,660	5,000
Net profit (loss) before tax	1,000	1,000	(400)
Cost of sales	6,500	7,000	8,000
Purchases	2,500	2,800	3,000
Taxation	500	500	nil
Finished goods at beginning of year A	1,400		

YEAR C

STATEMENT OF SOURCE AND APPLICATION OF FUNDS

	£'000
Source of funds	
Funds generated from operations	
Loss before taxation	(400)
Adjustment for items not involving the movement of funds	
Depreciation	1,500
	1,100
Taxation paid	500
Total funds generated from operations	600
Increase in bank overdraft	2,200
Increase in creditors	600
Increase in loan stock	1,500
Decrease in raw materials	1,100
	£6,000
Application of funds	
Purchase of freeholds	1,000
Purchases less disposals of plant and machinery	2,000
Increase in work in progress	100
Increase in finished goods	2,000
Increase in debtors	900
	£6,000

Our short analysis of the balance sheet will be as follows;

YEAR C

	£'000		£'000
Debtors	3,200	Bank	4,000
Stock	5,100	Creditors	1,200
	8,300		5,200
		Loan stock	3,600
			8,800
Freeholds	4,000	Cash	2,000
Plant and machinery	6,000	Reserves	7,000
Fixtures etc.	500	Profit and loss account	1,000
	£18,800		£18,800

This analysis of one year shows an adequate amount in net current assets with the amount for debtors being well in excess of creditors. There is some substantial borrowing from the bank and from loan stock holders but the total is below that for proprietors' funds.

However, as we have three years of figures available we will set them out in a comparative form in order to compare the figures year by year. This is a method to be much preferred for other than simple balance sheets as a much better overall view is obtained, as will be seen.

The comparative analysis can be set out in a variety of ways but perhaps it is better for bankers who are lending on overdraft to concentrate on the current liabilities and the current assets and put these items first when listing the liabilities and assets. After the balance sheet figures have been listed it is usual to note down any important figures from the profit and loss account which should be brought to attention. These would include turnover, the profit, the tax, a note of any extraordinary items of significance and the directors' remuneration. This last figure shows how much the directors are taking out of the business and can be related to the success or otherwise of the business. It is also useful to have noted the amount of the net current assets, the carry forward on the profit and loss account and the net worth.

COMPARATIVE FIGURES

	Year A £'000	Year B £'000	Year C £'000
Liabilities and Capital			
Current liabilities			
Bank	1,500	1,800	4,000 large increase
Creditors falling due within one year			
Trade	400	500	600
Others	600	600	600
Total current liabilities	2,500	2,900	5,200
Creditors falling due after one year			
Loan stock		1,500	3,000 increase
Others		100	600 ditto
	2,500	4,500	8,800
Proprietors funds			
Capital	2,000	2,000	2,000
Reserves	7,000	7,000	7,000
Profit and loss account	900	1,400	1,000 decrease year C
	£12,400	£14,900	£18,000
Assets			
Current assets			
Stocks			
Raw materials	1,200	1,700	600 large decrease
Work in progress	500	600	700
Finished goods	1,500	1,800	3,800 large increase
Debtors			
Trade	1,500	1,700	2,800 large increase
Others	400	600	400
Total current assets	5,100	6,400	8,300
Fixed assets			
Freeholds	1,800	3,000	4,000 increasing
Plant and machinery	4,000	4,500	6,000 ditto
Fixtures etc.	1,500	1,000	500 decreasing
	£12,400	£14,900	£18,800
Turnover (sales)	£12,000	£14,000	£15,000
Net profit before tax	1,000	1,000	(400)
Tax	500	500	nil
Net profit after tax	500	500	(400) loss year C
and after			
Extraordinary items	nil	nil	nil
Directors' remuneration	135	150	170
Net current assets	2,600	3,500	3,100
Carried forward	900	1,400	1,000
Net worth	9,900	10,400	10,000

The differences year by year are easily seen when the figures are set out in this form and this, obviously, must be an improvement on the simple analysis when only one year is considered.

The figures show that substantial extra borrowing has taken place and that there has been some capital expenditure. The profit record is not good even though turnover has been increasing. Debtors have risen sharply in the last year as has the amount in finished goods, whereas the amount in raw materials has diminished to a substantial extent.

A study now of the Statement of Source and Application of Funds will confirm these observations and show how the increase in funds available in year C was used.

Is there any more to be achieved by looking at the ratios? Let us make the calculations and see what they reveal.

CALCULATION OF RATIOS

	Year A	Year B	Year C
Rate of Gross profit $\dfrac{\text{Gross profit} \times 100}{\text{Sales}}$	$\dfrac{4{,}000 \times 100}{12{,}000} = 33.3\%$	$\dfrac{4{,}660 \times 100}{14{,}000} = 33.3\%$	$\dfrac{5{,}000 \times 100}{15{,}000} = 33.3\%$
Rate of Net profit $\dfrac{\text{Net profit} \times 100}{\text{Sales}}$	$\dfrac{1{,}000 \times 100}{12{,}000} = 8.3\%$	$\dfrac{1{,}000 \times 100}{14{,}000} = 7.1\%$	$\dfrac{400 \times 100}{15{,}000} = 2.6\%$
Current Ratio $\dfrac{\text{Current assets}}{\text{Current liabilities}}$	$\dfrac{5{,}100}{2{,}500} = 2.0$	$\dfrac{6{,}400}{2{,}900} = 2.2$	$\dfrac{8{,}300}{5{,}200} = 1.6$
Rate of stock turnover $\dfrac{\text{Average stock of finished goods} \times 365}{\text{Cost of sales}}$	$\dfrac{1{,}450 \times 365}{6{,}500} = 81 \text{ days}$	$\dfrac{1{,}650 \times 365}{7{,}000} = 86 \text{ days}$	$\dfrac{2{,}800 \times 365}{8{,}000} = 127 \text{ days}$
Debtor ratio $\dfrac{\text{Trade debtors} \times 365}{\text{Sales}}$	$\dfrac{1{,}500 \times 365}{12{,}000} = 45 \text{ days}$	$\dfrac{1{,}700 \times 365}{14{,}000} = 44 \text{ days}$	$\dfrac{2{,}800 \times 365}{15{,}000} = 68 \text{ days}$
Creditor ratio $\dfrac{\text{Trade creditors} \times 365}{\text{Purchases}}$	$\dfrac{400 \times 365}{2{,}500} = 58 \text{ days}$	$\dfrac{500 \times 365}{2{,}800} = 65 \text{ days}$	$\dfrac{600 \times 365}{3{,}000} = 73 \text{ days}$
Debtors/Creditors $\dfrac{\text{Trade Debtors}}{\text{Trade Creditors}}$	$\dfrac{1{,}500}{400} = 3.75$	$\dfrac{1{,}700}{500} = 3.4$	$\dfrac{2{,}800}{600} = 4.6$
Return on Capital employed $\dfrac{\text{Net profit before tax} \times 100}{\text{Average of shareholders' funds}}$	$\dfrac{1{,}000 \times 100}{9{,}650} = 10.3\%$	$\dfrac{1{,}000 \times 100}{10{,}150} = 9.8\%$	$\dfrac{(400) \times 100}{10{,}200} = (3.9\%)$
Gearing $\dfrac{\text{Loans}}{\text{Net worth}}$	$\dfrac{1{,}500}{9{,}900} = .15$	$\dfrac{3{,}300}{10{,}400} = .31$	$\dfrac{7{,}000}{10{,}000} = .70$

We can see from these calculations that although the gross profit percentage has been maintained the net profit percentage has dropped considerably. (It will be necessary to examine the items in the profit and loss account to determine why this has occurred.) The current ratio is satisfactory enough but the rate of turnover of finished stock has slowed considerably. As we have already noticed from the comparative figures and the statement of source and application of funds that the stock has increased considerably, whereas the amount in raw materials has much reduced, it will be necessary to enquire into the reasons for the variations in the levels of the different types of stock and for the slowing down of the rate of turnover.

Although the amount of debtors is well above that for creditors both debtor and creditor ratios have lengthened. We will wish to know if the terms of trade have altered dramatically or if there is some other reason.

The return on capital is now a minus quantity and the gearing ratio shows that additional loans have been taken and they will, of course, have to be serviced. Where will the funds for this come from if there is no profit?

The comparative figures and the statement of source and application of funds show clearly that extra sources of funds have been used to purchase more fixed assets and to increase the stock of finished goods. The ratios show that some important questions must be asked about the current assets, the current liabilities and the trading position even though the short analysis form for year C indicated that the net current assets were apparently satisfactory.

A full analysis in this way will enable a banker to prepare the appropriate questions to obtain a full understanding of the accounts.

VII

Inflation
No real understanding of accounts can be obtained without considering the effects of inflation. If there is a high rate of inflation in one year and money thereby loses its value, a comparison of two years' accounts cannot be accurately made without making an adjustment for inflation.

Similarly, when lower rates of inflation persist for several years comparison of trends over a period will be distorted. Unfortunately, inflation does not affect the prices of all items in the same way. Governmental control can be tried in an effort to minimize the effects of inflation and although this may have some short-term effect, larger price increases take place when the controls are lifted or prove ineffective. By contract or custom the prices of some goods and services are slower to react to changing conditions than others. Adjusting one year's accounts by a uniform percentage to account for inflation will not therefore give a true picture. For example, for several years residential property prices were reasonably steady and then in one year alone rose by several times the rate of the rise in the retail price index. There have been many attempts by the accountancy bodies to devise a system of inflation accounting but there have been difficulties in obtaining widespread acceptance of the various proposals.

The last attempt was by means of the issue of the Statement of Standard Accounting Practice No. 16 (SSAP 16) which for a few years became operative for annual accounting periods commencing after 1st January 1980. However, towards the end of 1985 so few companies were complying with this Standard of Accounting Practice that the Accounting Standards Committee bowed to the inevitable and withdrew the Standard saying that they were unable to get companies to comply by means of persuasion and if the government wished businesses to provide inflation adjusted accounts it would have to introduce legislation.

SSAP 16 was the result of several years of trying to put together a system of inflation adjusted accounts known as Current Cost Accounting (CCA) as opposed to Historic Cost Accounting (HCA) and a brief look at the proposals should enable a banker to see some of the areas where adjustments for inflation should be made in the figures which he now sees in HCA form.

The adjustments which had to be made were as follows:

1. *Depreciation adjustment*
Under HCA the amount written off as depreciation is a proportion of the cost price of the asset, but under CCA the proportion written off was related to the replacement cost of the asset. It will be appreciated that if the

replacement cost rises each year it is necessary not only to write off the additional annual amount, but also to bring up to date the amounts previously written off which have been calculated on a lower replacement cost. This is known as 'backlog depreciation'. The additional depreciation written off annually under CCA was therefore a combination of the extra annual depreciation plus the backlog depreciation.

2. *Cost of sales adjustment (COSA)*
When prices are rising sales of goods produce additional income but part of this difference between original cost and eventual sale price is not a normal trading income, but has been caused by inflation. COSA separated from the total profit that portion relating to rising prices caused by inflation.

3. *Monetary working capital adjustment (MWCA)*
As the adjustments relating to stocks of goods and sales of them (COSA) dealt with only one item which made up the working capital of the business, the remaining items, debtors, creditors, cash or overdraft, were adjusted by calculating the additional or reduced finance required by changes in prices, e.g. when prices are rising, more working capital is necessary to maintain the same volume of business.

These adjustments were made with the help of index numbers relating to the particular type of assets for the business concerned.

Gearing adjustment
It will be seen that although these three adjustments altered the trading figures, they relate to particular sections of the balance sheet. The depreciation adjustment related to the fixed assets of the business, whereas COSA and MWCA dealt with the working capital. The remaining items in a balance sheet are those for shareholders' funds (capital reserves and profit and loss account) and medium- and long-term borrowing. These items finance the net operating assets of the business (i.e. fixed assets plus working capital). Borrowing on medium or long term is generally repaid in fixed monetary amounts and in inflationary times there is an advantage to the borrower. The amount of the advantage will depend upon the proportion of funds borrowed to those provided by the shareholders. The three adjustments we have mentioned had the effect, when prices were rising, of reducing the HCA profit, but the full reduction brought about by these adjustments would only be applicable if the shareholders had provided all the funds to finance the net operating assets. It was not necessary to provide for the full reductions if part of the finance to support the net operating assets was medium- or long-term borrowing. In this case the adjustments were reduced by the proportion applicable to the borrowed moneys.

The advantage of borrowing money in inflationary times could be seen clearly if the amount applicable to the gearing adjustment was compared with the interest payable. This is the way in which the gearing adjustment had to be shown in the accounts.

Adjustments to the balance sheet
Under the CCA system, assets in the balance sheet had to be shown at their value to the business at current price levels. This was not easy to achieve with accuracy as subjective judgement had to be reached by whoever did the valuation. However, in times of inflation, if other considerations balance each other out, fixed assets increase in price and their value to the business was shown by an increase in the figures stated in the balance sheet. This produced a surplus and the contra entry to such surplus was shown as a current cost reserve. The contra entries to the adjustments shown to the profit and loss account were also made in the current cost reserve.

The effect of CCA
Although CCA was not a complete system of accounting for inflation it was a help to directors and managers of businesses. It showed in the profit and loss account that extra funds had to be retained to preserve the value of the business entity. This reduced the profit that was available for distribution. The value of the business entity would not, therefore, be endangered by the inadvertent paying of excessive dividends which would have depleted the company's net assets.

The banker's view
From a banker's point of view all additional information is of interest and the additional figures produced by CCA helped to give a banker a better understanding of the strengths and weaknesses in balance sheets.

A banker, however, cannot ignore the effects of inflation on a balance sheet and a profit and loss account just because inflation adjusted accounts are not produced. He must use his common sense and make mental adjustments for such matters as;
   (1) turnover which should increase by more than the rate of inflation if the business is progressing.
   (2) depreciation of plant and machinery. Replacement will probably cost more than the original cost of existing assets. Is the depreciation rate sufficient to cover this?
   (3) other fixed assets. Have the values altered greatly from those shown in the balance sheet?

71

(4) expenses of running the business. Is inflation sending them out of control?

(5) Are the financing arrangements and the interest being paid satisfactory to the needs of the business and working in its favour?

These and other points will occur to alert bankers examining balance sheets and they should be able to make shrewd judgements even though inflation adjusted accounts are not made available.

An example is as follows;

CASE 11

JONES SMITH AND CO. LTD.

Engineers

	£		£
Debtors	27,000	Creditors	24,000
Stock	37,000	Bank	5,000
Work in progress	14,000	Corporation tax—3 months	6,000
Local Authority Loans	10,000	Dividends	4,000
		Directors' loans	20,000
	88,000		59,000
		Corporation tax—15 months	8,000
		Mortgage	30,000
			97,000
Freeholds	50,000	Capital	60,000
Plant and machinery	40,000	Reserves	30,000
Fixtures and fittings	7,000	Profit and loss account	6,000
Motor vehicles	8,000		
	£193,000		£193,000
Sales	£250,000	Profit	£12,000
		after	
		tax	£8,000
		depreciatiion	£3,000
		directors' remuneration	£15,000

This is a relatively small company.

There are many indices produced for inflation rates for various goods and services. They all have advantages and disadvantages but possibly the most useful one is the retail price index. For this example, we will assume that this index showed an increase of 10 per cent. in the year covered by the accounts. We would expect, therefore, the sales figure to be at least 10 per cent. up on the previous year, if only to reflect the same volume of sales. As for the debtors and creditors, these items are at approximately 1/10th of sales, and debtors exceed creditors. This is a perfectly healthy position and, although the value of debtors when collected will be less as the value of money will have dropped, a similar reversed situation will arise over creditors and one will offset the other.

Borrowing money in an inflationary period is of advantage to the borrower as repayment is made with depreciated money and if we look at the liabilities of the company it has the advantage of borrowing from the bank, from the directors and also on mortgage. It also has the use of the amount of its corporation tax liabilities on terms equivalent to interest-free loans for 3 months and 15 months. If the mortgage is a long-term mortgage, the company will be having a considerable advantage if we assume that inflation to some extent will continue year by year.

Turning now to the assets side of the balance sheet, we have already dealt with debtors. The amount of stock and work in progress seems high when related to sales. Too much money tied up in these items is wasteful of a company's resources but in times of high inflation and expected further price rises, additional stock bought before the rise in price can be a worthwhile investment. The only point to consider is whether the company can afford to make the investment; in this case it can.

The investment in the local authority loan may not be wise if looked at in isolation as normally such loans are at fixed interest rates. It may be, however, that the investment is a temporary one and the money has been put aside for a particular purpose. There would be no gain from the inflation point of view of using the funds to repay the mortgage. It would be preferable to retain the long-term mortgage if use can be made of these funds in due course.

The balance sheet figure for freeholds will have to be compared with the figures shown for this item in previous years. If no additional purchases have been made and the freeholds are in the accounts at original cost they could well be worth much more when considered at up-to-date prices. The retail price index would not be an accurate index to use for making this comparison but a banker's knowledge of how property values have moved will enable him to make an estimate of the present value. If a more accurate figure is required a valuer will have to be consulted. The result of an increased figure being put upon the freeholds will be to increase the proprietor's funds on the other side of the balance sheet.

Plant and machinery are fixed assets, as are freeholds, but cannot be considered in the same way. These fixed assets wear out much more quickly than freeholds, and enhanced values cannot be put on them year by year. There will come times when machinery has to be replaced and it is the replacement value which is important when considering the effects of inflation. The normal depreciation of an asset merely provides for the value of the asset less any residual value to be written off during its useful life. The funds so retained in the business will be sufficient only to cover the original cost of the asset, whereas a replacement asset will probably cost a much greater amount. Companies should, therefore, look ahead to the time when replacement will be necessary and see that they do not so deplete themselves of resources that they will find it difficult to finance the replacements. Normal depreciation is, therefore, insufficient and a company is in danger of overstating the amount of its distributable profits if it makes no adjustment for eventual replacement of the depreciating assets.

In the example, we see that depreciation of only £3,000 has been made on fixed assets ignoring freeholds of £55,000. This must surely be insufficient and enquiry of the company about this seems necessary.

Profits at £12,000 after tax will have been overstated but as these profits have not been fully distributed (dividends take £4,000) a sizeable retention has been left in the business. A banker will be unlikely to know the replacement cost of individual items of equipment and the customers will have to be consulted. It must be kept in mind though that it is unusual to replace machinery by exactly similar articles. Improvements in machines take place and when the time comes it will most probably mean that a better model will be required at a further increased price.

Similar reasoning is appropriate also for fixtures and fittings although the figures involved are generally very much smaller. Replacement cost must also be taken into account on motor vehicles, and here again the increases in price over the years have not been in line with increases in the retail price index. All a banker can do is keep a watch on the prices of vehicles and he will then have an idea as to the eventual replacement cost. The effective life of motor vehicles in business enterprises is relatively short and a banker will have to consider whether the amount put aside for depreciation is adequate.

A banker must not overlook the effect of inflation on the profit and loss account and the net profit which emerges. If a certain amount of stock in trade costs £100 and because of inflation the same amount of stock costs £110 to replace three months later, there are two effects. The first is the obvious one—the business will require more funds to finance the same physical volume of trade. The second is the effect on the profit ratio. If a mark-up of 20 per cent. is usual in the trade the sale price on the original purchase price would be £120. If the sale price is related to the cost at the time of sale and the sales of this stock took place at the end of the period, the sale price would be £132 and the additional £12 would be due to inflation. In practice, sales generally take place over a period and the effect is therefore not so marked, but it is clear that the difference between the actual sales figure and the original purchase price will overstate the true profit figure. Part of the profit is due to inflation alone and will be needed for the purchase of replacement stock at prices increased by inflation. Unfortunately, corporation tax is assessed on profits unadjusted for inflation. As such profits are overstated, the excess corporation tax assessed on these profits denudes businesses of essential working capital. A banker must therefore keep in mind that there should be, as a minimum, adequate profits—after deduction for tax and dividends—retained in the business to increase the working capital to the extent that:

(1) the physical level of business activity is maintained and

(2) the company is able to deal with the replacement of assets when necessary.

In all, it will be seen that the values placed on items in the balance sheet can be considerably distorted by inflation and that variations for each type of asset or liability must be considered separately. Also, because of the eventual larger replacement costs of both fixed assets and stock, the profit shown is very likely to be overstated by using accounts which are unadjusted for the effects of inflation. It is only from profits, both past and future, that sufficient resources are generated to provide for replacement of both assets and stocks at inflated prices. By ignoring this aspect of inflation, accounts prepared on an historic cost basis overstate net profits.

VIII

Forecasting

We have, so far, been concentrating on the interpretation and analysis of past performance as a guide to the assessment and control of banking advances.

However, the advances which are required by borrowers are for a future period and it would, of course, ease the lot of the banker if a crystal ball would tell him how a borrower's profit and loss account and balance sheet would appear for this future period.

The nearest we can get to this is to ask the borrower to provide a forecast. However, forecasts are rarely pessimistic and it is amazing how many people with poor annual accounts can produce forecasts which would please the most optimistic of businessmen.

Therefore, let there be a word of warning. The past record is fact and indicates whether a borrower is able to make a success of his business or not. The forecast is not fact and the results have to be proved in practice.

This is not to say that forecasts are of no use. This is far from the case and the production of forecasts is now required more often by bankers. They are of particular use when monitoring difficult accounts as problems are seen more quickly than is the case when a banker waits for a balance sheet to alert him to trouble.

We have considered profit and loss accounts, balance sheets, and statements of source and application of funds and all these accounts can be put in forecast forms. A business can start with its estimate of profit for the forthcoming period and this can be backed with details of every aspect of the business and not just conjured up. Subsequently capital expenditure will have to be taken into account and then the forecast balance sheet and the forecast statement of source and application of funds can be prepared.

However, a banker's advance is not in plant and machinery or in debtors but is in cash and what he wants to know is how the banking account will work during the financial period.

For this purpose an additional statement is required, being the Cash Forecast or Cash Flow Forecast which is a forecast showing how much cash will come into and go out of the banking account on a monthly or quarterly basis.

A typical forecast in a simplified form is as follows:

CASE 12

MARTIN DAY LTD.

CASH FORECAST FOR 6 MONTHS

	Jan	Feb	March	April	May	June
Inflows	£	£	£	£	£	£
Debtors	12,000	12,000	12,000	14,000	16,000	18,000
VAT refund		2,000			2,300	
Sale of machinery			7,000	17,000		
	12,000	14,000	19,000	31,000	18,300	18,000
Outflows						
Rent, rates and insurance	500	500	500	500	500	500
Wages etc.	4,000	4,000	4,000	4,000	4,000	4,000
General overheads	2,000	2,000	2,000	2,000	2,000	2,000
Payments to creditors ...	8,000	8,000	8,000	8,000	8,000	8,000
Bank charges			1,500			1,500
New machinery					15,000	
	14,500	14,500	16,000	14,500	29,500	16,000
Net for month	(2,500)	(500)	3,000	16,500	(11,200)	2,000
Bank balance b/fwd	(10,000)	(12,500)	(13,000)	(10,000)	6,500	(4,700)
Bank balance c/fwd	(12,500)	(13,000)	(10,000)	6,500	(4,700)	(2,700)

It will be seen from this forecast that the highest overdraft will be about £13,000 in February and that the account should be in credit for a time in April. We cannot be sure of the estimated bank balance as this will depend upon when the actual payments and receipts appear in the banking account. However, the company accountant will be able to help with this aspect.

Obviously with a forecast such as this a banker will be more in touch with the activities of the business and will not, for example, be led to think, when April comes, that the company must be doing well whereas the credit balance will be the result of a sale of machinery and not of trading.

The banker should check that the forecasts are not inconsistent with past experience and in the course of time will know whether or not the company's forecasts are reliable.

Subsequently regular actual figures should be submitted by the company and compared with the estimates; explanations for substantial variations should be sought.

It will be seen that in order to make estimates the starting point must be with past actual figures. An understanding of such figures is therefore vital and this is why the interpretation of balance sheets is important for lending bankers.